MW01234911

Contents of Book

This book consists of stories and pictures of the life of Lieutenant Colonel William Henry Davis and his family. William Henry Davis was born in 1747 and died in 1818.

Information has been collected through many various sources including family letters, cemetery searches, military records and information gathered through various historical societies throughout the United States. Some of the other sources of information have been through Find a Grave.com and Ancestory.com.

Research back in the 1700's and 1800's can be difficult due to lack of record keeping and censes. I have tried very hard to make sure that all information in this book is accurate based on the information that has been gathered.

Contents of Book

Branches listed in the book are the children of William Henry Davis. He had 11 (eleven) children.

Twigs listed in the book are the grandchildren of William Henry Davis. He had 51 grandchildren.

Splinters listed in the book are great-grandchildren of William Henry Davis. He had 277 great-grandchildren.

Branches, Twigs and Splinters of Lieutenant Colonel William Henry Davis

1747-1818

Branches = Children

Twigs = Grandchildren

Splinters = Great Grandchildren

Lieutenant Colonel William Henry Davis
1747– DOB
May 14, 1818 – DOD

William Davis was the son of
Edward and Lucy Davis. He was born in
1747 in Dinwiddie County, Virginia. William
Davis was a Revolutionary War Soldier.
William married Agnes Lanier on August 29,
1769 in Brunswick, Virginia per records.
Agnes was born between the years of 1750-
1752 and she died on February 21, 1813 in
Wilkes County, Georgia. Agnes's father was
Sampson Lanier who was born in 1712 and
died September 2, 1757 in Brunswick County,
Virginia. Her mother was Elizabeth
Chamberlain who was born in 1715 in
Brunswick County, Virginia and died in 1780.

William and Agnes had 11 children.
All of the following children were listed in
William Davis's Last Will and Testament.
The children were **Edward,** William Thomas,
James Sherwood, Elizabeth, Charles, Joshua,
Lucy, Samuel, Lewis Lanier, Micajah
Washington and Baxter Burwell Davis.

Lieutenant Colonel William Davis was
in the Fifth Virginia Regiment in the
Revolutionary War and was at the Surrender
of Cornwallis at Yorktown. Documents show

that William Davis's income was 60 (sixty) dollars a month during war time.

An original document from the New York Public Library from the book <u>Georgia Baptists: Historical and Biographical</u> by Jesse Harrison Campell reads: "At sixteen years of age, though much against the will of his friends, Mr. Davis volunteered as a soldier of the revolution, and was sometime under the command of General LaFayette. He was wounded in the head, and suffered greatly from fatigue, and hunger. While the army of LaFayette was on a forced march to join Washington in the capture of Cornwallis, young Davis was without a morsel of food two whole days. This kindness, on the part of LaFayette, was remembered with gratitude all his life. He was heard to mention it in his last sickness. He was present at the surrender of Cornwallis, and after the war, returned to his family in Virginia."

He moved from Virginia to Wilkes County, Georgia around the year 1795. William and Agnes settled down near Sardis Church about ten miles north of west from Washington. William had received a military grant for 990 acres of land on Long Creek in Wilkes County from the State of Georgia on November 2, 1807.

William lived in Georgia in a little town named Washington. This little town was named in honor of President George Washington and was incorporated as a town in 1780.

Lieutenant Colonel William Henry Davis and his wife, Agnes Lanier Davis, are buried at Sardis Baptist Church Cemetery in Wilkes County Georgia.

- *Excerpted from the article by Robert (Rel) Davis:*

Lost Graves of Agnes Lanier and William Davis 1747-1818

by Robert (Rel) Davis, c. 2008

Some years back I began a journey to find my family's roots. From the north Texas hills where I was born, back to west Georgia, farther back to eastern Georgia, and then back to southern Virginia, I noticed one striking similarity among the terrain of each locale: Low, rolling hills and wooded valleys and meandering creeks. It was as if each generation that went a'roaming was seeking a place that "looked" like home. And "home" was never mountains or prairies or seashores. It was rolling hills and small streams.

Somewhere along my personal journey, I decided to find the graves of my great-great-great-great grandparents, **William Davis** and **Agnes Lanier**.

They started out in South Virginia but after the War (the

Revolutionary War, of course) they headed west, settling on land **William** received for his service in the Revolution. This was in Wilkes County, Georgia, along the old Indian trail that led southwest from Virginia in those days, near the town of Washington, now as then the county seat. Family records had them buried in Sardis Baptist Church.

My brother and I arranged to meet in Washington, GA, one spring morning and make a pilgrimage to our ancestors' grave sites. He drove down from the District of Columbia and I drove up from Florida. After a brief visit to the local library, we headed west by northwest along Route 78 for the small community of Rayle, GA.

Just north of Rayle we found the church, a white spire-peaked building resting on seven acres of wooded land - in rolling hills and next to a tiny creek. No one was around. The cemetery sprawled out north and west of the church building. Behind the church to the east is another white building, obviously used for Sunday School.

We began wandering the area looking for the gravestones of our ancestors. Most of the cemetery was composed of newer graves - after 1850. Off to one side we found some of the older ones, in varying stages of repair. But search as we might, we could not find the grave markers for William and Agnes.

Finally , a car drove up to the church property and a young woman and two small children got out. She was, it turned out, doing some clerical work that day. She knew nothing about any old gravestones, however, but suggested we talk to Josephine, the church historian. She provided a phone number and we called. Josephine Wilson Orr was home and would be delighted to meet with us.

Another drive for a couple of miles along farm-to-market roads brought us to the Orr place. She was a storehouse of information. She had even written a book about the church history, and she graciously gave us a copy.

There were two problems, however. First, the initial record book for the church -

from 1788 when it was founded until 1804 - had been lost. William and Agnes had moved to Georgia around 1795, so the record of their joining is no longer in existence. The records of their burials, on the other hand, were available since they passed away in 1818 and 1813 respectively.

Which leads to problem number two. In 1959, the old Rayle school house was to be abandoned and the church bought the building from the county board of education. It was moved to its present location behind the church building, and placed on top of the original cemetery, "since there were no markers and no one knew who was buried there." Our ancestors are buried somewhere underneath the Sunday School building!

I suppose it is understandable, of course. Those were pioneer days. Gravestones in Europe had traditionally been made of slate. In those areas in the New World where slate was not readily available, wooden markers were usually used - sometimes "temporarily" until slate could be imported from the Old World. In 150 years, the wooden markers would have long ago disintegrated.

And, of course, all the children of William and Agnes left Wilkes County for places farther west. Not one descendant remained in the area. There was no one to tend their graves or replace their grave markers.

Why? Why did all 11 of their children leave the place where their parents passed away? There could be several reasons. One, most of the children had been born in Virginia, so Wilkes County, GA wasn't really their home in the first place. Second, this was a time of great migration. Young people wanting to make their fortune would naturally want to continue the westward march. There was land to claim (or to take from the Indians) in plenty - farther west.

Sardis Baptist Church Cemetery
Wilkes County, Georgia

Agnes Lanier Davis
Sardis Baptist Church Cemetery
Wilkes County, Georgia

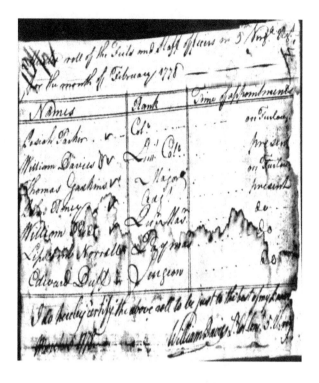

Document signed by William Davis---bottom of document

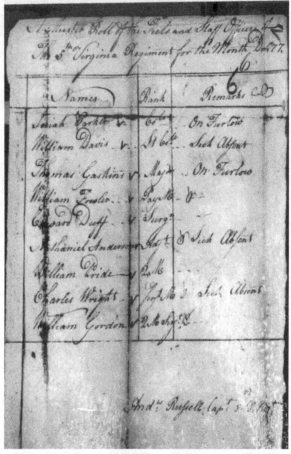

December 1777 – Muster Roll
William would have been between
29-32 yrs old

In the name of God. Amen

I, **William Davis** of the County
and State aforesaid knowing the certainty of
death, do make, ordain and establish the
following instrument of writing as my last
will and testament (being blessed with usual
health and of sound mind and memory). To
wit, first I give and bequeath to my son
Edward Davis the property which he has
already received from my Estate together with
one dollar **{about $20 in 2007}** to be paid him
by my executors in twelve months after my
decease in full of his legacy.

2nd I give to my son **William Davis** the
property he has already received from my
estate together with one dollar to be paid by
my executors in twelve months after my
decease in full of his legacy.

3rd I give to my son **James Davis** the
property he has already received from my
estate together with one dollar to be paid him
by my executors in twelve months after my
decease in full of his legacy.

4th I give to my son **Charles Davis** the
property he has already received from my
estate together with one dollar to be paid him

by. my executors in twelve months after my decease in full of his legacy.

5th I give to my daughter **Elizabeth** the property she has already received from my estate also one dollar to be paid her by my executors in twelve months after my decease in full of her legacy.

6th I give to the lawfull heir or heirs of my daughter **Lucy** the property heretofore received by her in full of my legacy which might be claimed from my estate in her behalf.

7th I give to my son **Joshua Davis** the property he has already received from my estate, also one dollar to be paid him by my executors in twelve months after my decease in full of his legacy.

8th It is my will and desire that all my just debts should be as speedily discharged as conveniently may be by my executors who are hereby authorized to dispose of such personal property belonging to my estate as they may conceive can be best spared for that purpose.

9th It is my will and desire that the residue of my estate not disposed of in the foregoing articles or items should be distributed amongst my four youngest sons in the following manner, to wit that **Samuel Davis** and **Lewis Lanier Davis** shall each of them choose for themselves one Negro apiece from amongst the whole of my Negroes.. The tract of land whereon I now live I wish to be equally divided between my two youngest sons, **Micajah Washington Davis** and **Baxter Boxwell Davis**. I also wish my youngest son, **Baxter Boxwell Davis**, to have a certain Negro boy by the name of Will. The whole of the residue of my estate consisting of Negroes, stock, household furniture, etc. Etc. it is my will and desire that it should be equally divided amongst my four youngest sons to wit, **Samuel Davis, Lewis Lanier Davis, Micajah Washington Davis** and **Baxter Bockwell** {sic} **Davis.**

Lastly I do hereby constitute and appoint to this my last will and testament **Joshua Davis** and **Lewis Lanier Davis** and **George Willis** as executors hereby revoking all former wills made by me.

In testimony whereof I have hereunto set my hand and seal this 28 day of July in the year of our Lord one thousand eight hundred and thirteen.

Signed sealed and delivered in presence of us
Wm. Brook
Claybrook Williamson
Wm.
Evans

    WILLIAM DAVIS (L. S.)
William Brook, Claybrook Williamson and Wm. Evans, the three subscribing witnesses to

the foregoing Will came into open court and
made oath that they saw William Davis sign
and seal and acknowledge the foregoing to be
his last will and testament, that at the time of
his so doing he was of sound and disposing
memory and that they subscribed their names
as witnesses by his express direction.
Sworn to in open court - Claybrook
Williamsonthis
  6th July 1818 Wm. Brook John
Dyson, Evans
Recorded the 14th of July 1818.

Washington-Lanier ancestry of Mary Gibson Jones established by family and official records, viz:—

1. John Washington married Mary Flood (Blount Fford) Dans county, Virginia.
2. Their son, Richard Washington, married Elizabeth Jordan of Virginia.
3. Their daughter, Elizabeth Washington, married Sampson Lanier, of Virginia.
4. Their son, Sampson Lanier, married Elizabeth Chamberlin, of Virginia.
5. Their daughter, Agnes Lanier, married William Davis, of Virginia.
6. Their son, Lewis Lanier Davis, married Louisa Tucker Irvine, of Georgia.
7. Their daughter, Caroline Davis, married Sanders W. Faver, of Georgia.
8. Their daughter, Louisa Ann Faver, married Joel W. T. Gibson, of Coweta county, Georgia.
9. Their daughter, Mary Gibson, married Thomas J. Jones, M. D., of Georgia.

IRVINE, IRVIN, IRWIN

Ancestry, established by family and official records, and "The Irvines and their Kin"—By L. Boyd.

She is descended from William Irvine, son of Robert Irvine and Margaret Wylie, one of the seven brothers who came to America about 1730. William Irvine married Anne Craig, who was of noble blood, in Ireland; she died and was buried in the churchyard of Raloo, by the side of her daughter, Johanna, who had previously died. William and his two sons, Christopher and David, came to America. They landed at Philadelphia, Pa., and afterwards removed to Bedford county, Virginia, and were among the first settlers on Burden's grant. David Irvine married Jane Kyle of Bedford county, Virginia, and went to Kentucky; and Christopher Irvine married (1) Louisa Tucker of Amherst county, Virginia, two sons by this marriage, Isaiah Tucker and Charles; his wife died and he married (2) Prudence Echols of Virginia, six children by this marriage. This Christopher Irvine is a descendant of Christopher Irvine who commanded the light house for King James IV. at the Battle of Flodden Field, or as Sir Walter Scott, in "Mar-

Branches = Children
Of Lieutenant Colonel
William Henry Davis

11 Children

Edward Davis 1770-1849
William Thomas Davis 1772-1823
Elizabeth Davis 1773
Charles II Davis 1774
James Sherwood Davis 1775-1851
Joshua Davis 1782-1847
Samuel Davis 1785-1850
Lucy Davis 1787-1818
Micajah Washington Davis 1789
Lewis Lanier Davis 1797-1833
Baxter Burwell Davis 1799-1870

Edward Davis
First child of William Henry Davis
1770 estimated – DOB
September 2, 1849 – DOD

Edward Davis was the son of William and Agnes Lanier Davis. Edward married Dorothy Margaret Mason who was born in South Carolina around the year 1779. Margaret and Edward were married in 1796. Edward also married a lady by the name of Margaret Noble. It is unclear as to which Margaret he married first.

Edward Davis was a blacksmith and he owned a saloon. He was known to have an ugly temper.

Edward's children were William, James, Isaac B., Daniel, John, Burwell, Ransom, Margaret, Martha, Presley, Mary Polly, Matthew, James, Elizabeth, Susanna Jane and John Henry Davis.

Margaret Noble was blind in her elder years of life. She died in Pleasant Hill, Alabama on April 28, 1854. Edward Davis is buried in Dallas County, Alabama.

William Thomas Davis
Second child of William Henry Davis
1772 – DOB
December 1, 1823 – DOD

William Thomas Davis was the son of William and Agnes Lanier Davis. William Thomas was born in Mecklenburg, Virginia in 1772. In 1791, he married Mary Gresham. Mary Gresham was born in 1771 and died in 1824.

Per records, William Thomas and Mary Gresham had the following children: Elizabeth, James Gresham, Mary Christian Polly, William Owen, Nancy Ann Mourning, Judith Leake and Martha Frances Davis.

William Thomas Davis died on December 1, 1823 in Jones, Georgia.

**Elizabeth Davis
Third child of William Henry Davis
1773 – DOB**

**Charles Davis II
Fourth child of William Henry Davis
1774 – DOB – in Brunswick County,
Virginia**

James Sherwood Davis
Fifth child of William Henry Davis
September 7, 1775 – DOB
March 4, 1851 – DOD

James Sherwood was the son of William and Agnes Lanier Davis. James Sherwood was born in Mecklenburg, Virginia on September 7, 1775. In 1800, he married Judith L. Gresham. Judith L. Gresham was born in 1780 and died in 1860.

Per records, James Sherwood and Judith had the following children: Mary Gresham, Catherine, James Gresham, John C., William Columbus, Elizabeth, Harriett L., Tabitha Frances, Sarah Jane, Joshua LT, and Judith Agnes Davis.

In the 1840 United States Federal Census, James Sherwood Davis was listed as a residence of Harris County, Georgia.

James Sherwood Davis died on March 4, 1851 in Whitesville, Harris, Georgia.

Joshua Davis
Sixth child of William Henry Davis
November 29, 1782 – DOB
December 28, 1847 – DOD

Joshua Davis was the son of William and Agnes Lanier Davis. Joshua was born in Brunswick, Virginia on November 29, 1786. On January 10, 1811, he married Martha Patsy Trammell. Martha Patsy Trammell was born in 1792 and died in 1872.

Joshua Davis served in the War of 1812 as a Private in Captain Adam Heath's Company of Infantry, Third Regiment Georgia State Troops from September 26, 1814 to March 2, 1815.

After their marriage, Joshua and Martha Patsy moved to Fayette County, Georgia, then to Coweta County, Georgia and then to Heard County, Georgia. In Heard County, they first settled near the mouth of Hillabahatchee Creek on what is known as the Glover place. They then settled about nine miles northwest of Franklin on Lot 85 in the 12th district of Carroll County now known as Heard County. Joshua and Martha built a log cabin in this portion of Carroll County, later to become a part of Heard County. According to Dr. James Bonner's A Short History of Heard County, " The Joshua Davis home was designated as the first seat of government in

Heard County as no court house existed and Franklin wasn't incorporated until 1831. Joshua and Patsy Davis lived here from 1830 till his death in 1847. The cabin still stands today and is located about 12 miles from Franklin, Georgia.

Per records, Joshua and Martha Patsy had the following children: James Chamberlain, Mary Amanda, Lewis Franklin, William Thomas, Martha Emiline (Lina), Rebecca Balsora, Sarah Sophronia (Fronie), and Wilson Lumpkin "Lummie" Davis.

A letter written by Rebecca Davis Lawley states; "Joshua and Martha Davis were truly Heard County pioneers. They settled after the Creek Indian lands were ceded, felled trees to build a home and gained sustenance from the land. The sixth generation of Davis's live on original Joshua Davis land today. Joshua and Martha Davis are buried in raised box-tombs in the Davis-Ridley Cemetery located approximately 7 miles west of Franklin, Georgia off Frolona Road." They are buried on Lot 85.

MARRIAGE LICENSE.

To any Judge, Justice of the Peace, or Minister of the Gospel:

YOU ARE HEREBY AUTHORIZED TO JOIN

Joshua Davis and *Patsy Trammel*

in the Holy State of Matrimony, according to the Constitution and Laws of this State, and for so doing this shall be your License.

And you are hereby required to return this License to me with your Certificate hereon of the fact and date of the Marriage.

Given under my hand and seal, this 14th day of Jany 1811

D. Terrell Cek (SEAL.)

Ordinary.

CERTIFICATE.

GEORGIA, WILKES COUNTY.

I CERTIFY THAT *Joshua Davis*

and *Patsy Trammel* were joined in Matrimony by me,

this 10th day of Jany 1811 Nineteen Hundred and

M. Reeves —

Recorded this 18th day of Feby 1930

R. O. Burkala Ordinary.

**Marriage Certificate of Joshua Davis
and Martha Patsy Trammell
January 10, 1811**

Joshua Davis
Davis-Ridley Cemetery - Georgia

Old Joshua Davis Home Place

Restored Joshua Davis Home Place

Samuel Davis
Seventh child of William Henry Davis
1785 – DOB – Mecklenburg County, Virginia
Abt. 1850 – DOD

Samuel Davis was the son of William and Agnes Lanier Davis. Samuel married Elizabeth Bennett. Elizabeth was born in 1795 and died in 1850. Per records, Samuel had one child by the name of Richard Bines Davis.

Samuel Davis died around 1850.

Lucy Davis
Eighth child of William Henry Davis
1787 – DOB
1818 – DOD

Lucy Davis was the daughter of William and Agnes Lanier Davis. On January 25, 1817, Lucy Davis married William Henderson. William Henderson was born around 1780. Lucy Davis Henderson died in 1818 only one year after she was married. No children are recorded.

Micajah Washington Davis
Ninth child of William Henry Davis
1789 – DOB

Lewis Lanier Davis
Tenth child of William Henry Davis
1794 – DOB
December 23, 1833 – DOD

Lewis Lanier Davis was the son of William and Agnes Lanier Davis. Lewis Lanier was born in 1794 in Brunswick County, Virginia. On September 10, 1818, he married Louisa Tucker Irvine. Louisa Tucker Irvine was born in 1803 and died in 1860.

Per records, Lewis Lanier and Louisa Tucker Davis had the following children: Caroline Amelia, Ann Cordella, Isaiah Tucker, William L., Andrew J., Isabella, and Nancy Davis.

Lewis Lanier Davis died on December 23, 1833 in Wilkes County, Georgia.

MARRIAGE LICENSE.

To any Judge, Justice, or other person authorized by law:

YOU ARE HEREBY AUTHORIZED TO JOIN

Lewis L. Davis and *Louisa J. Irvin*

in the Holy State of Matrimony, according to the Constitution and Laws of this State, and for so doing this shall be your License.

And you are hereby required to return this License to me with your Certificate hereon of the fact and date of the Marriage.

Given under my hand and seal, this *7th* day of *Sept.* 1818

John Bynum Clk. (SEAL)

Ordinary.

CERTIFICATE.

GEORGIA, WILKES COUNTY.

I CERTIFY THAT *Lewis L. Davis,*

and *Louisa J. Irvin* were joined in Matrimony by me,

this *10th* day of *Sept.* 1818 Nineteen Hundred and

Malachi Reeves V.D.M.

Recorded this day of

Ordinary.

Marriage Certificate of Lewis Lanier Davis and Louisa Tucker Irvine – September 10, 1818

Baxter Burwell Davis
Eleventh child of William Henry Davis
1799 – DOB
After 1870 – DOD

Baxter Burwell Davis was the son of William and Agnes Lanier Davis. Baxter Burwell was born in 1799 in Brunswick, Virginia. On January 18, 1808, he married Unity Christmas Power in Warren County, North Carolina. Unity Christmas Power was born in 1789 and died in 1830.

Baxter Burwell Davis died sometime after 1870.

Twigs = Grandchildren
Of Lieutenant Colonel
William Henry Davis

51 Grandchildren Recorded

William Davis 1787-1862
James Davis 1795
Isaac B. Davis 1798-1856
Daniel Davis 1799-1869
John Davis 1800
Burwell Davis 1801
Ransom Davis 1802-1850
Margaret Davis 1804-1877
Martha Davis 1807
Presley Davis 1810-1863
Mary Polly Davis 1812-1870
Matthew Davis 1814
James Davis 1817-1880
Elizabeth Davis 1819
Susanna Jane Davis 1824-1899
John Henry Davis 1833-1911
Elizabeth Davis 1793-1859
James Gresham Davis 1796-1846
Mary Christian Polly Davis 1800-1831
William Owen Davis 1800-1847
Nancy Ann Mourning Davis 1802-1887

Ju0dith Leake Davis 1804-1878

Martha Frances Davis 1813-187

Mary Gresham Davis 1798-1850

Catherine Davis 1803-1845

James Gresham Davis 1806-1867

John C. Davis 1806-1867

William Columbus Davis 1809-1886

Elizabeth Davis 1811-1882

Harriett L. Davis 1813

Tabitha Frances Davis 1815

Sarah Jane Davis 1818-1892

Joshua LT Davis 1823-1867

Samuel 1824-1867

Judith Agnes Davis 1826-1872

James Chamberlain Davis 1812-1812

Lewis Franklin Davis 1817-1857

Mary Amanda Davis 1818-1849

William Thomas Davis 1820-1860

Martha Emiline (Lina) Davis 1823-1898

Rebecca Balsora Davis 1826-1905

Sarah Sophronia Davis 1830-1904

Wilson Lumpkin Davis 1833-1914

Richard Bines Davis 1817-1891

Caroline Amelia Davis 1819-1899

Ann Cordella Davis 1820-1872

Isaiah Tucker Davis 1822

William L. Davis 1824

Andrew J. Davis 1826

Isabella Davis 1828

Nancy Davis 1829

William Davis
Child of Edward Davis
Grandchild of William Henry Davis
January 10, 1787 – DOB per gravestone
November 1, 1862 - DOD

William Davis was the son of Edward and Dorothy Margaret Mason Davis. He was born in South Carolina in 1787. His wife, Elizabeth Duncan Davis, was born in Georgia in 1809 and died in 1900. William and Elizabeth married around 1830. Both William and his wife Elizabeth were born during the **Colonial Period**. Their oldest child was born in Alabama in the **Antebellum Period** of 1830's.

Per records, William and Elizabeth had the following children: Emily, Nancy, Margaret Livador, Elizabeth, Edward, Jane, Samuel Webster, Franklin M., Martha A., Presley, William Marshall and Sarah Lucinda Davis.

William and his wife, Elizabeth, are buried in the old Davis family cemetery which is located just south of Troy, Alabama in Pike County.

**William Davis – Davis Family
Cemetery in Troy, Alabama**

**James Davis
Child of Edward Davis
Grandchild of William Henry Davis
1795 – DOB
Died in Dallas County, Alabama**

Isaac B. Davis
Child of Edward Davis
Grandchild of William Henry Davis
1798 – DOB
March 21, 1856 – DOD

Isaac B. Davis was the son of Edward Davis. Isaac was born in 1798 in Pendleton District, South Carolina. On November 15, 1821, Isaac married Arrensy Pior. On February 16, 1851, Isaac married Harriett P. Farrow in Jefferson, Georgia.

Per records, Isaac B. Davis had the following children: William P., Wylanty P., Narcissa Malinda, Hezakiah Kirah, Anderson, Celestia Lisa, Alfred, Ansley, Isaiah, James and Lavina Davis.

Tax Digest records from Jefferson County, Georgia recorded that by the year 1853, Isaac B. Davis owned 1405 acres and 16 slaves for a total value of $22,882 dollars.

Isaac B. Davis died on March 21, 1856 in Alabama.

• Jefferson Co., GA Tax Digest records, Volume I
Records in name of Isaac B. Davis

Survey of 490 acres on Reedy Creek for William Matthews in 1815 recorded in office

of Probate Court, Plat Book 1, page
177. Name of Isaac Davis appears on the plat.

1822— 77TH. District, Capt. Noah Turner's
Isaac B. Davis-Jefferson Co., 400 acres,
grantors – Jane Neely & others;
adjoining William Barr; Brushy Creek
watercourse; 1 slave.

Isaac B. Davis – Appling Co., 490
acres, grantor – No. 155, 2 district.
1824— 77th. District, Capt. Turner.
Isaac B. Davis-Jefferson Co., 400 acres,
(no grantor or adj. info), Brushy Creek
watercourse; 6 slaves.

Isaac B. Davis-Jefferson Co., 200 acres,
adjoining J. Matthews; Brushy Creek
watercourse.

Isaac B. Davis-Appling Co., 490 acres;
adjoining-#155, watercourse-2.

1826— 77th. District, Capt. Ross
Isa ac B. Davis-Jefferson Co., 400 acres,
adjoining Barr, Brier Creek
watercourse; 14 slaves.

Isaac B. Davis-Jefferson Co., 200 acres,
adjoining Rogers, Brier Creek
watercourse.

Isaac B. Davis-Appling Co., 490 acres.
Isaac B. Davis-Early Co., 250 acres.

1830— 77th District.
Isaac B. Davis-Jefferson Co., 600 acres; adjoining Bass; Brushy Creek watercourse; 17 slaves

Isaac B. Davis – Jefferson Co., 184 acres; grantor Briggs; adjoining Young; Brushy Creek.

Isaac B. Davis – Appling Co., 490 acres; adjoining-155, water course

Isaac B. Davis- Early Co., 250 acres; adjoining 191, watercourse 11.

Isaac B. Davis – as adm' of estate H. Pior – Warren Co., 304 acres; adjoining Adams on Brier Creek; 4 slaves.

1834— 77th. District, Capt. Gunn.
Is aac B. Davis-Jefferson Co. 870 acres; adjoining Allen, Brushy Creek Watercourse; 17 slaves.

Isaac B. Davis-Jefferson Co., 184 acres; adjoining Lowry; Brushy Creek watercourse.

Isaac B. Davis-Early Co., 250 acres; grantor Brown; adjoining-171, watercourse 11.

Isaac B. Davis-Appling Co., 490 acres; grantor Rowe; adjoining 155, watercourse 2.

1836— 77th. District, Capt. Gunn.
Is aac B. Davis-Jefferson Co., 1291 acres, adjoining Lafever; Brushy Creek watercourse; 17 slaves.
Isaac B. Davis-Appling Co., 490 acres.
Isaac B. Davis-Early Co., 250 acres; Brushy Creek watercourse.

Isaac B. Davis for Robert Prior—490 acres in Appling Co., adjoining 190, watercourse 5.

1846— 77th. District.
Isaac B. Davis-Jefferson Co., 1303 acres, 16 slaves, value-$11.35. (I assume this value means value of acreage).

Isaac B. Davis-Appling Co., 1190 acres.

Isaac B. Davis-Randolph Co., 202 ½ acres.

Isaac B. Davis-Early Co., 250 acres,

1853— 77th. District.

Isaac B. Davis-Jefferson Co., 1405 acres, 16 slaves, value $22,882

Isaac B. Davis as Grd. For James W. Hudson, 2 slaves, $1630

MARRIAGE OF ISSAC B DAVIS AND ARRENSY PIOR
NOVEMBER 15, 1821

Isaac Davis and Arrensy Pior

GEORGIA)
Jefferson County)

THESE are to authorize and permit you to join in the Honorable state of MATRIMONY Isaac Davis of the one part, and Arrensy Pior of the other part, according to the rites of your church, provided there be no lawful cause to obstruct the same, and this shall be your authority for so doing.

Given under my hand as Clerk of the Court of Ordinary of the County aforesaid, this 16th day of November 1821 -

To any Minister of the Gospel, Judge, Justice of the) Robt P. Shelman, Clk
Inferior Court, or Justice of the Peace to celebrate.)

....

I DO hereby certify that I joined Isaac Davis and Arrensy Pior and were joined together in the Holy Bonds of Matrimony by me, on the same day of the month 15th Nov 1821

Daniel Connel J.P

_____

Isaac Davis & Arrensy Pior

GEORGIA,
          County)

Know all men by these Presents, that we Isaac Davis & James Wright are held and firmly bound unto the Court of Ordinary of the Jefferson County, in the sum of Eight Hundred and Fifty-seven Dollars and Fourteen Cents, to which payment well and truly to be made, we bind ourselves, our heirs, executors and administrators, jointly and severally by these Presents, sealed with our seals, and dated this fifteenth day of November 1821 -

THE CONDITION of the above obligation is such, That whereas there is a marriage intended to be solemnized between Isaac Davis and Arrensy Pior

Now, If there be no lawful cause to obstruct the same, then this obligation to be void, else to remain in full force and virtue.

Signed, sealed and acknowledged)
          in the presence of   )   James Wright L.S.

N Shelman J.J.Ct.   Isaac Davis L.S.

MARRIAGE OF ISSAC B DAVIS AND HARRIETT P FARROW
FEBRUARY 16, 1851

Mr. Issac B. Davis and Miss Harriet Farrow

GEORGIA, Jefferson County

To any Minister of the Gospel, Judge, Justice of the Inferior Court,
or Justice of the Peace;

You are hereby authorized to join Mr. Issac B. Davis and Miss Harriet Farrow in the
Holy State of Matrimony, according to the Constitution and Laws of this State; and for
so doing this shall be your sufficient license.

GIVEN UNDER MY HAND AND SEAL, this Twelfth day of February 1851

Nicholas Diehl C.I.C.

GEORGIA, Jefferson County.

I do Certify, That Mr. Issac B Davis and Miss Harriet Farrow were duly joined in
Matrimony by me, this 16th day of February 1851
Sterling G. Jordan J P

Dr. Daniel Davis
Child of Edward Davis
Grandchild of William Henry Davis
May 1, 1798 – DOB
July 12, 1869 – DOD

Dr. Daniel Davis was the son of Edward Davis. Daniel was born on May 1, 1798 in Pendleton District, South Carolina. Dr. Daniel Davis married Melanie (Lanie) Brownlee of Abbeville District, South Carolina. Melanie (Lanie) Brownlee was born on March 29, 1799 and died on October 10, 1880.

Dr. Daniel Davis received his education while in South Carolina. In 1818, Daniel and Melanie moved to Alabama and then later settled in Tuscaloosa County in the year 1821. Daniel Davis was of the Baptist faith.

Per records, Dr. Daniel Davis and Melanie Brownlee had the following children: Edward, Dr. Elias, Ralph, Mary B., Edward Lee, Amanda, Mary Gresham, William B., Harriett L., Judith Agnes, Elizabeth Jane (Bettie), Joshua LT, Lanie Ann and John Martin Davis.

Dr Daniel Davis died in Jefferson County on July 12, 1869.

John Davis
Child of Edward Davis
Grandchild of William Henry Davis
1800 – DOB – South Carolina

Burwell Davis
Child of Edward Davis
Grandchild of William Henry Davis
1801 – DOB – South Carolina
Died in Dallas County, Alabama

Burwell Davis was the son of
Edward Davis. Per records, Burwell had one
daughter by the name of Mellissa Davis.

Ransom Davis
Child of Edward Davis
Grandchild of William Henry Davis
1802 – DOB – South Carolina
1850 – DOD – Dallas County,
Alabama

Ransom Davis was the son of Edward Davis. Per records, Ransom had the following children: Fereby, Mary, Nancy and William Davis.

Margaret Davis
Child of Edward Davis
Grandchild of William Henry Davis
April 3, 1804 – DOB – South Carolina
March 1, 1877 – DOD – Pike County,
Alabama

Martha Davis
Child of Edward Davis
Grandchild of William Henry Davis
1807 – DOB
Died in Florida

Presley Davis
Child of Edward Davis
Grandchild of William Henry Davis
July 4, 1810 – DOB
March 15, 1863 – DOD

Presley Davis was the son of Edward Davis. Presley was born on July 4, 1810 in Pendleton District, South Carolina. On November 29, 1831, Presley married Salina Ludlow. Salina was born in 1810 and died in 1872.

Per records, Presley and Salina Davis had the following children: James Franklin, Missouri, Malissa, Lila Ann (Zilly Ann), Margaret Ann, Amanda, Mary Elizabeth, Tennessee and Augustus C. Davis.

The following was a letter written by Presley Davis on August 12, 1857 and was published in The Independent American.

The Independent American

August 12, 1857

Mr. Editor:

It is known to your readers that I was a candidate in this county for Commissioners of Roads and Revenue, and was defeated in my election on last Monday. When I say that I am perfectly satisfied with the result, you and your readers, who personally know me, will have no hesitancy in believing; but I am at the same time mortified and dissatisfied with the base and dishonorable means employed by the opposition which produced that result. I am under many, and lasting obligations, to many of my good Democratic friends who sustained me, who refused to be made pliant tools of, by the whippers-in of that party, and I take this occasion to convey to them my sincere thanks. But to a portion of that party, who were busy in traducing my character, by circulating the grossest falsehoods against me, causing many of my own friends to desert me, I have to say of such, they have characters which no gentleman need to envy.

I was a member of the board of Commissioners for the three past years, and to the best of my ability, discharged my whole duty, but, to defeat my election, my action in that body was willfully and grossley misrepresented.

It was industriously circulated at several boxed in this county (evidently a concerted plan to defeat me), that I had cast my vote in favor of giving and allowing John T Moody, County

Superintendent of public schools, for his services, $500.00 an amount greatly too much for the services he had to render, and more than the law would allow. This is a falsehood which turned many from me. Now the facts which follows, I hold myself ready to prove and will do so should it become necessary. When the question of the salary for the above named officer was brought before the Commissioners Court, I addressed the balance of the Court, and stated to them, the law governing the case, that the amount to be paid Mr. Moody was left to the sound discretion of the Court, and that as a member of that Court, I should vote to pay Mr. Moody, for carrying out the letter of the law, and acted upon that idea myself. Mr. Darby, Mr. Simmons and myself were all present and voting, Mr Darby voted to allow Mr. Moody for his services $450.00. Mr Simmons voted for the sum of $400.00 and I voted for the sum of $300.00 and thus the vote upon the allowance stood, as no two of the Court agreed, and it became necessary for us to agree upon the amount, the ballance of the Court allowed me to change my former vote $300.00...and I did so under protest and voted for the next lowest sum $400.00 which fixed the salary for this year at that sum.

So, Mr. Editor, it will be seen that instead of wasting the people's money by voting for exorbitant salary to that officer, I did infact vote for a sum $100.00 less than any other member of the Court, and changed at last to save County money perhaps from paying a higher amount. Upon the circulation of this story many of my good friends were induced to vote against me, seeing as they thought, I was an unfaithful or disqualified guardian of the public interest. Of this sir, I complain, and hence, I feel it enjoined upon me to let the people know all the facts, while I may possibly reinstate myself in the confidence of those who believed the lie, and peradventure, cause the cheek of the liars to burn with shame and remorse. I desire to stand before the public on my own true merits, and although I may never again ask their suffrages, still I have a name, a character worth more to me, than any office within the gift of the people.

By the way, the office of County Superintendent in my opinion, should be abolichod; I have ever thought so, since I examined the law creating it. The duties assigned to that officer could be as well discharged by the Township Trustees (and in many instances much better), and in every Township there can be found men, who are so fully identified with the success of the free school system, who would without fee or reward, attend to the whole buisness, thus saving enough money in Pike County, in each year to pay the tuition of 150 poor children for one quarter. Allowing the average salaries of Superintendents to be $500.00.....and 52 counties in the state, it will be seen that these Superintendents alone, for what I hold to be valueless service, receive the large sum of $26,000.....or enough money to educate for one quarter, nearly 1000 poor children. And I trust the next legislature will abolish the office entirely. Entertaining these views, the people can see one reason I voted for Mr. Moody's salary to be fixed at $300.00 instead of $500.00 as was falsely charged against me

A strict defence of my conduct in the office they conferred upon me is the only apology I offer for thus appearing before them.

Very Respectfully
Presley Davis

The following are articles published in the Independent American in 1856 about Presley Davis.

- Independent American January 9, 1856

Mrs. Presley Davis of our town sent us some of the finest turnips we have ever seen. Three of them weighed just 21 1/2 pounds, the largest one of the three weighed 7 3/4 pounds. One of them measured 32 inches in circumference and the flavor when cooked would have tempted the most delicate appetite.

Independent American January 16, 1856

Mr. Presley Davis seeing in our last weeks paper that his wife had been sending us some mammoth turnips, undertook to furnish us with a larger specimen. Altho we are always on the side of the ladies, still we are compelled to acknowledge that Mr Presley Davis has furnished us with a larger, much larger specimen, one weighing 9 pounds.

The following is an article written in the Southern Advertiser on January 4, 1861 about Presley Davis.

Southern Advertiser January 4, 1861   Eggnog----Quitman Guards
On Friday last, our fellow townsman, Presley Davis invited the Quitman Guards, to visit him at his house, where he intimated that he would furnish them with the "creature comforts" so greatful to all who love to see Christmas roll around.
At dinner time, the Guards, under the command of Captain Gardner were escorted to the residence of Mr. Davis by that inimitable BRASS BAND, led by "Dan" who knows how to spread his "peacock" feathers on such occasion
We almost felt like wishing that Christmas would last always and Davis' nog and dinner would prove inexhaustible.

The following is an article written in The Southern Advertiser on March 25, 1863 about the death of Presley Davis.

The Southern Advertiser   March 25, 1863

Sad Affair

On Sunday evening, the 15th, as Mr. Presley Davis, of this place, was examining a mule of his, that appeared to be lame, from having been ridden the night before......the mule struck him with his hind foot, upon the breast and arm, breaking both, and so seriously damaging him, that he died in a very short time. Mr. Davis was an old citizen of this place, was highly esteemed and loved by his fellow townsmen, and by his upright course had won for himself a large circle of true friends. His death is a calamity upon the community and it will be long before his place can be filled by another such a man. We tender our sincere condolence to the family afflicted with such a heavy and irreparable loss.

The following is an article published in The Southern Advertiser on June 24, 1863 concerning the funeral of Presley Davis.

- The Southern Advertiser
June 24, 1863

The funeral of Mr. Presley Davis will be preached on the 4th Sabbath in this month by Rev. Mr. Dixon or Dickson at Beulah Church.

>>>>>>>In the mid to late 1800's, churches would have circuit preachers who would come around once a month. If a person died, they would be buried rather quickly and the funeral would be held when the circuit preacher arrived>>>>>>>>

Mary Polly Davis
Child of Edward Davis
Grandchild of William Henry Davis
1812 – DOB
1870 – DOD

Mary Polly Davis was the daughter of Edward Davis. Mary Polly was born in 1812 in South Carolina. On October 29, 1840, Mary Polly married Bryant McLeod. Bryant McLeod was born in 1812 and died in 1866.

Per records, Mary Polly and Bryant McLeod had the following children: William B., Susan, Zillian Ann, Caroline Saline, Sara Jane, Morgan M. and Frances McLeod.

Mary Polly Davis McLeod died in 1870 in Pike County, Alabama.

Matthew Davis
Child of Edward Davis
Grandchild of William Henry Davis
1814 – DOB

James Davis
Child of Edward Davis
Grandchild of William Henry Davis
1817 – DOB
May 20, 1880 – DOD

James Davis was the son of Edward Davis. James was born in 1817 in South Carolina. On August 1, 1839, James married Julia Ann McDonald in Dallas County, Alabama. Julia Ann was born in 1824 and died on October 24, 1890.

Per records, James and Julia Ann had the following children: Sarah Jane, Susan A., Mary Evelyn "Emily", Amanda, Clara F., James Jr., Allen and Yancy Davis.

James Davis died on May 20, 1880. James is buried at Cedar Creek Cemetery in Farmersville, Alabama.

Elizabeth Davis
Child of Edward Davis
Grandchild of William Henry Davis
1819 – DOB
Death in Dallas County, Alabama

Elizabeth Davis was the daughter of Edward Davis. Elizabeth was born in 1819 in South Carolina. On December 20, 1838, Elizabeth married George W. Overton. George was born in 1812.

Per records, Elizabeth and George had the following children: Thomas W., John F., James E., Sarah R., Lizzy R. and Martha G. Overton.

Elizabeth Davis Overton died in Dallas County, Alabama.

Susanna Jane Davis
Child of Edward Davis
Grandchild of William Henry Davis
December 12, 1824 – DOB
August 12, 1899 – DOD

Susanna Jane was the daughter of Edward Davis. Susanna was born on December 12, 1824, in Selma, Alabama. Susanna married William Mathis Grumbles. William was born in 1825 and died in 1901.

Per records, Susanna and William Grumbles had the following children: Edward Davis, Harriet Elizabeth, Margaret Keziah, Winnifred Armita, William Henry, Martha Ann, Mary Jane, Susan Caroline, Louisa Ann, Benjamin Franklin, Charles Glover, Thomas Green and Sarah Melissa Grumbles.

Susanna died in 1899 in Lytton Springs, Texas. Susanna is buried in Blalock Cemetery in Bastrop County, Texas. Her tombstone reads, "Weep not for me, but plant ye a tree in memory of me."

Susanna Jane and William Mathis Grumbles
1845

Susanna Jane Davis Grumbles
Blalock Cemetery in Bastrop County, Texas

William Mathis Grumbles
Blalock Cemetery in Bastrop County,
Texas

John Henry Davis
Child of Edward Davis
Grandchild of William Henry Davis
December 25, 1833 – DOB
February 18, 1911 – DOD

John Henry Davis was the son of Edward Davis. Henry was born on December 25, 1833, in Mobile, Alabama. On October 4, 1865, John Henry married Nancy Catherine Lee in Hays City, Texas. Nancy Catherine Lee was born on August 5, 1848 and died on September 11, 1920.

Per records, John Henry and Nancy Catherine Davis had the following children: William Franklin, John Noble, Nancy Avarillah, Thomas Mark, Reuben Marshall, Robert Shelton, Jerry Lee, Mary Cryssa, Authur Robertson, Ardelia May and Sarah Alta Davis.

John Henry Davis died on February 18, 1911 and is buried in Brown County, Texas.

o **John Henry Davis** was born in Mobile, Alabama in 1833. His grave marker states 1834, but it's 1833. His mother was born in South Carolina. Before she married John Henry's Father, her last name was **Noble**. She had at least 2 brothers, **John Noble**, born in South Carolina in 1795 & died in Hays County, Texas between 1871 &

1880. He was living with **John Henry Davis** and his family in Precinct 3 when he died, near Manchaca. The other brother was **Jessie Noble**. No more information on him at this time.

○　　　John Henry's mother died from Yellow fever and his father married again. He raised another family. His father had at least 2 more sons by his second wife. **John Henry Davis** had at least 1 brother. When John Henry's family is found in Alabama they can be traced to his father's two families. **John Henry Davis' Father** was a blacksmith and owned a saloon. He was known to have a very bad temper.

○　　　My grandfather, **William Franklin Davis,** saw him and one of his sons by his second wife. His son was a big man. My mother says he moved to Texas near Austin. My grandfather was never in Alabama, so he had to be in Texas when my grandfather saw him. My mother says he is buried near Austin or in Brown Co., Texas. She can't remember. His first family was small people. Second family was much larger. His son by his 2nd marriage was just a few years older than my grandfather. Mom says she thinks he had 3 sons and 1 daughter by his second wife.

Written by Grandson of William F. Davis

1910
John Henry Davis
Nancy Catherine Lee Davis
Arthur Robertson Davis
Lois Gladys Marshall is holding
Lonnie Paul Marshall. The other
child is Nettie Opal Marshall

John Henry Davis, Mary Crissie with her two small children and Ardelia Mae Davis – 1908 10 miles South East of Brownwood, Texas

John Henry is seated in the middle.
To his right is Nancy Catherine Lee
Davis. The tallest man is Edgar A.
Marshall; the woman to the far right
is Nancy Avarillah Davis Marshall.
The man next to Edgar Marshall is
William Franklin Davis. The two
girls standing are Ardelia Mae Davis
(next to Nancy) and Mary C. Davis.
The child Nancy Catherine is holding
is thought to be Sarah Alta who was
the Davis's youngest child. The
other men are Davis sons but which
is which is unknown.
1894 – Llano County, Texas

William S. Lumbley and John Henry Davis

Nancy Catherine Lee Davis – 1891

NANCY LEE
DAVIS
1848-1920

Nancy Catherine Lee Davis
Wife of John Henry Davis

John Henry Davis

DEATH RECORD

PLACE OF DEATH

Death Certificate of John Henry Davis

Elizabeth Davis
Child of William Thomas Davis
Grandchild of William Henry Davis
1793 – DOB
March 1859 – DOD

Elizabeth Davis was the daughter of William Thomas Davis. Elizabeth was born in 1793 in Jones County, Georgia. In 1810, Elizabeth married Reuben Bennett. Reuben Bennett was born in 1787 and died in 1821. In 1816, Elizabeth married Henry Benjamin Cabaniss. Henry Cabaniss was born in 1775 and died in 1850.

Per records, Elizabeth Davis had the following children: Reuben Jr., Thomas and Mary Elizabeth Bennett.

Elizabeth died in March of 1859 in Floyd, Georgia.

James Gresham Davis
Child of William Thomas Davis
Grandchild of William Henry Davis
January 31, 1796 – DOB
June 15, 1846 – DOD

James Gresham Davis was the son of William Thomas Davis. James was born in 1796 in McIntosh, Georgia. On August 17, 1815, James married Martha Harvey in Jasper, Georgia. Martha was born in 1796 and died in 1845.

Per records, James and Martha had the following children: Harvey, Elizabeth, Nancy, Mary, Samantha Agnes, William Edwin, Thomas L., Martha F., Mariah and James H. Davis.

James Gresham Davis died on June 15, 1846 in Jenkins, Georgia.

Mary Christian Polly Davis
Child of William Thomas Davis
Grandchild of William Henry
Davis
1800 – DOB – Jones County,
Georgia
May 24, 1831 – DOD

William Owen Davis
Child of William Thomas Davis
Grandchild of William Henry Davis
1800 – DOB
November 2, 1847 – DOD

William Owen Davis was the son of William Thomas Davis. William was born in 1800 in Jones County, Georgia. On December 22, 1824, William married Elizabeth Watts McDaniel. Elizabeth was born in 1810 and died in 1869.

Per records, William and Elizabeth had the following children: William Thomas, James S., Mary Ann Elizabeth, Jacob Emmissy, John R., Joseph Julius, Sarah Agnes and Benjamin Franklin Davis.

- Union County Tax records show that W.O. Davis estate had 453 acres, valued at $1359 in 1848. He had 4 slaves under age 60 years old and their value was $1925

William Owen Davis died in 1847 in Union County, Arkansas.

Nancy Ann Mourning Davis
Child of William Thomas Davis
Grandchild of William Henry Davis
April 4, 1802 – DOB
September 2, 1887 – DOD

Nancy Ann Mourning Davis was the daughter of William Thomas Davis. Nancy Ann was born in 1802 in Jones County, Georgia. On April 29, 1824, Nancy married Orrin Alston Beck in Jones County, Georgia. Orrin Alston was born in 1803 and died in 1868.

Per records, Nancy Ann and Orrin Alston had the following children: William, John Thomas, Joshua Emasy, Mary Frances, Fredonia Ann, Darthula Mary, Judge, Morning C., Orrin Alston Jr. and James Owen Beck.

Nancy Ann Mourning Davis Beck died on September 2, 1887 in Benton County, Mississippi. She is buried in the Beck Family Cemetery.

**Nancy Ann Mourning Davis
Beck
Beck Family Cemetery**

Judith Leake Davis
Child of William Thomas Davis
Grandchild of William Henry Davis
1804 – DOB
1878 – DOD

Judith Leake Davis was the daughter of William Thomas Davis. Judith was born in 1804 in Jones County, Georgia. On September 11, 1823, Judith married Samuel McDaniel. Samuel was born in 1802 and died in 1846.

Per records, Judith and Samuel had the following children: Martha, Sarah Agnes Mary Elizabeth, Thomas Marley, Edwin, William, Samuel and John T. McDaniel

Judith Leake died in 1878 in Alascosa, Texas.

Martha Frances Davis
Child of William Thomas Davis
Grandchild of William Henry Davis
1813 – DOB
June 1, 1870 – DOD

Martha Frances Davis was the daughter of William Thomas Davis. Martha was born in 1913 in Jones County, Georgia. On January 4, 1827, Martha married John Franklin Stewart. John Franklin was born in 1800 and died in 1863.

Per records, Martha and John Franklin had the following children: Isaac Newton, Mary Ann, Jonathan Milton, Martha E., Wiley D., Charles J., Joseph Wiley and William Franklin Stewart.

Martha Frances died on June 1, 1870 in Randolph County, Alabama.

Mary Gresham Davis
Child of James Sherwood Davis
Grandchild of William Henry Davis
1798 – DOB
1850 – DOD

Mary Gresham Davis was the daughter of James Sherwood Davis. Mary was born in 1798 in Wilkes County, Georgia. In 1818, Mary married George Benjamin Davis. George was born in 1796 and died in 1873.

Per records, Mary and George had the following children: Martha Gresham and James Benjamin Davis

Mary Gresham Davis died in 1850.

Catherine Davis
Child of James Sherwood Davis
Grandchild of William Henry Davis
1803 – DOB
1845 – DOD

Catherine Davis was the daughter of James Sherwood Davis. Catherine was born in 1803 in Fayette County, Georgia. On July 31, 1823, Catherine married Allen Post. Allen was born in 1799 and died in 1876.

No children are recorded for Catherine Davis. Catherine died in 1845 in Coweta County, Georgia.

James Gresham Davis
Child of James Sherwood Davis
Grandchild of William Henry Davis
September 23, 1806 – DOB
September 19, 1867 – DOD

James Gresham Davis was the son of James Sherwood Davis. James was born in 1806 in Fayette County, Georgia. On May 27, 1828, James married Ronah Matthews. Ronah was born in 1806 and died in 1890.

Per records, James and Ronah had the following children: Henry, John Marion, Roxie Ann, Adolphus Dakota, William Calloway and George Granberry Davis.

James Gresham Davis died in 1867 in Harris County, Georgia.

John C. Davis
Child of James Sherwood Davis
Grandchild of William Henry
Davis
September 23, 1806 – DOB – in
Georgia
September 19, 1867 – DOD –
Harris, Georgia

William Columbus Davis
Child of James Sherwood Davis
Grandchild of William Henry Davis
January 5, 1809 – DOB
October 15, 1886 – DOD

William Columbus Davis was the son of James Sherwood Davis. William was born in 1809 in Fayette County, Georgia. On February 22, 1825, William married Malissa Gold. Malissa was born in 1805 and died in 1827. Children born to William and Malissa were William Gold Davis and Narissa Davis.

On December 18, 1827, William married Martha C. Reeves in Fayette County, Georgia. Martha was born in 1810 and died in 1860. William and Martha had the following children: Elizabeth B., James W., George Washington, Martha Jane, Mary Amanda, William B., Thomas B., Victoria B., and Laura Elizabeth Davis.

On October 25, 1860, William married Miranda Frances Myers in Nacogdoches, Texas. Miranda was born in 1836 and died in 1869. Children by William and Miranda were Frances Murneva and Henry C. Davis.

On July 22, 1870, William married Mary Jane Joiner in Cherokee County, Texas.

Mary Jane was born in 1837 and died after 1880. Mary Jane was listed in the 1880 U.S. Census records. William and Mary Jane had the following children: John B., Leroy, Joshua and Christopher Columbus Davis.

William died in 1886 in Van Zandt, Texas.

Elizabeth Davis
Child of James Sherwood Davis
Grandchild of William Henry Davis
April 5, 1811 – DOB
December 28, 1882 – DOD

Elizabeth Davis was the daughter of James Sherwood Davis. Elizabeth was born in 1811 in Jasper County, Georgia. In 1828, Elizabeth married John R. Jones in Georgia. John was born in 1800 and died in 1896.

Per records, Elizabeth and John had the following children: Elizabeth, Catherine, Dr. Charles Gresham, William Calloway, Mary D., Thomas, Harriet J., Julia E., Benjamin J. and Tip Jones.

Elizabeth died in 1882 in Woodberry, Meriwether, Georgia.

Harriett L. Davis
Child of James Sherwood Davis
Grandchild of William Henry
Davis
1813 – DOB

Harriett L. Davis was the daughter of James Sherwood Davis. Harriett was born in 1813 in Harris County, Georgia. In 1833, Harriett married William A. Calloway. No children are recorded for Harriett L. Davis.

Tabitha Frances Davis
Child of James Sherwood Davis
Grandchild of William Henry Davis
1815 – DOB

Tabitha Frances Davis was the daughter of James Sherwood Davis. Tabitha was born in 1815 in Georgia. On January 26, 1838, Tabitha married Freeman W. Hadley in Harris County, Georgia. Freeman was born in 1800.

Per records, Tabitha and Freeman had the following children: Judith Ann, Eleanor Ellen, Joseph Davis, Thomas, Jonas and John J. Hadley.

Tabitha Frances Davis Hadley died in Marshall County, Alabama.

Sarah Jane Davis
Child of James Sherwood Davis
Grandchild of William Henry Davis
April 29, 1818 – DOB
December 23, 1892 – DOD

Sarah Jane Davis was the daughter of James Sherwood Davis. Sarah was born in 1818. On October 6, 1835, Sarah married James Lyle in Coweta County, Georgia. James was born in 1811 and died in 1899.

Per records, Sarah Jane and James had the following children: Charles G., Elizabeth E., Mary Jane, James Davis "Jim", Margaret, Martha Ann, Missouri M., Berryman Erastus, Isabelle Eunice, William Franklin, Richard C., Judith and Thomas Milton Lyle.

Sarah Jane Davis Lyle died in 1892 in Tremont, Itawamba County, Mississippi. She is buried at Mt. Pleasant Methodist Cemetery in Itawamba County, Mississippi.

JANE DAVIS LYLE
APR. 29, 1818
DEC. 23, 1892

Sarah Jane Davis Lyle – Mt Pleasant Methodist Cemetery in Mississippi
Joshua Davis
Child of James Sherwood Davis
Grandchild of William Henry Davis
1823 – DOB
1867 - DOD

Samuel LT Davis
Child of James Sherwood Davis
Grandchild of William Henry Davis
1824 – DOB
September 19, 1867 – DOD

Samuel LT Davis was the son of James Sherwood Davis. Samuel was born in 1824 in Fayette County, Georgia. Samuel married Sarah Jane Mullins. Sarah was born in 1825.

Per records, Samuel and Sarah had one child by the name of Thomas S. Davis.

Samuel Davis died in 1867 in Harris County, Georgia.

Judith Agnes Davis
Child of James Sherwood Davis
Grandchild of William Henry Davis
1826 – DOB
1872 – DOD

Judith Agnes Davis was the daughter of James Sherwood Davis. Judith was born in 1826 in Fayette County, Georgia. In 1847, Judith married Marshall Scoggins.

No children are recorded for Judith Agnes. Judith died in 1872 in Georgia.

James Chamberlain Davis
Child of Joshua Davis
Grandchild of William Henry Davis
November 4, 1812 – DOB – Wilkes, Georgia
November 4, 1812 – DOD – Wilkes, Georgia

Mary Amanda Davis
Child of Joshua Davis
Grandchild of William Henry Davis
July 4, 1818 – DOB
October 11, 1849 – DOD

Mary Amanda Davis was the daughter of Joshua Davis. Mary was born in 1818 in Wilkes County, Georgia. On March 1, 1832, Mary married Paschal Harrison Taylor in Heard County, Georgia. Paschal was born in 1807 and died in 1879.

Per records, Mary and Paschal had the following children: William F., John B., Martha Serepta, Oliver, James Paschal, Owen Harrison, Mary Ann, Peter and Shady A.J. Taylor.

Mary Amanda died in 1849 in Randolph County, Alabama.

Mary Amanda Davis Taylor

Lewis Franklin Davis
Child of Joshua Davis
Grandchild of William Henry Davis
March 1, 1817 – DOB
February 5, 1857 – DOD

Lewis Franklin Davis was the son of Joshua Davis. Lewis was born in 1817 in Wilkes County, Georgia. On January 28, 1841, Lewis married Elizabeth Anne Pittman. Elizabeth was born in 1822 and died in 1888.

A few years after their marriage, they settled in Heard County, Georgia, about 7 miles northwest from Franklin on lots 48 and 49 of the 12th District of Carroll County.

Per records, Lewis and Elizabeth had the following children: Martha Melissa, Nancy Diana, Mary Elizabeth, Martin Joshua, William Owen, Lewis Franklin "Dock" Jr., Emily Teresa "Emma", James Thadeus "Jim", George Pittman and Andrew Smith Davis.

Lewis Franklin Davis occupied a log home at the present site of Owen C. Davis Sr. home. Lewis died of injuries sustained in a log rolling. Elizabeth continued to operate the farm and became known for her managerial skills.

Lewis died in 1857 in Heard County Georgia. Lewis and his wife, Elizabeth, are both buried in the family burial ground on Lot 85 near the old residence of Joshua Davis

Lewis Franklin Davis

William Thomas Davis
Child of Joshua Davis
Grandchild of William Henry Davis
January 22, 1820 – DOB
After 1860 – DOD

William Thomas Davis was the son of Joshua Davis. William was born in 1820 in Wilkes County, Georgia. On September 11, 1845, William married Temperance Jane "Tempe" Awbrey in Heard County, Georgia. Temperance was born in 1827 and died in 1860.

Per records, William and Temperance had the following children: L. Thomas, James A. and Elizabeth Davis.

William Thomas Davis died after 1860 in Georgia.

Martha Emiline (Lina) Davis
Child of Joshua Davis
Grandchild of William Henry Davis
July 13, 1823 – DOB
February 9, 1898 – DOD

Martha Emiline (Lina) Davis was the daughter of Joshua Davis. Martha was born in 1823 in Georgia. On June 1, 1843, Martha married Ales Ridley in Heard County, Georgia. Ales was born in 1806 and died in 1886.

Per records, Martha and Ales had the following children: twin daughters that died in infancy, Saphronia Balsora, William Franklin, Warren Ales, Martha Ella, William Davis, Polly Smith and Alice Lee Ridley.

Martha Emiline died in 1898 in Heard County, Georgia.

Rebecca Balsora Davis
Child of Joshua Davis
Grandchild of William Henry Davis
September 5, 1826 – DOB
October 26, 1905 – DOD

Rebecca Balsora Davis was the daughter of Joshua Davis. Rebecca was born in 1826 in Heard County, Georgia. On August 27, 1846, Rebecca married William Alphonso Pittman. William was born in 1817 and died in 1904.

Per records, Rebecca and William had the following children: James Franklin, Joshua Martin, Martha Elizabeth "Sis", William Alfonso Jr., Nancy Smith "Nan", William Alphonso II, William Owen, Jefferson Davis, Etta Jane and Addie Balsora Pittman.

Rebecca Balsora died in 1905 in Randolph County, Alabama.

• Letter from Wm Alphonso Pittman to his son J F Pittman, Confederate Soldier in 1865 - http://familytreemaker. genealogy.com/users/l/e/e/Davis-E-Lee/index.html. For this letter I want to thank The Davis Lee Family Home Page, created by Davis Emerson Lee

A father writes his soldier son in this, the third letter lent The Press by Mrs. Pearse Seegar. The writer, W. A. Pittman, is the recipient of the first letter, written from Texas in 1858 and published in this paper three weeks ago. It is thought that the Jef Davis mentioned here is the younger son, the father of Misses Eris and Lucy Pittman and Mrs. Owen Ford, now living in the Springfield community.

At Home, January the 13, 1865

Dear Dear Son,

I received yours of the 5 of January, which gave me great satisfaction to learn that you was well. These few lines leavs myself with the rest of the family well at this time, hopeing these few lines may find you enjoying the same blessing. I was glad to hear that you was at Talladega. I was fearful that you had bin sent Mobeal.

Thare has nothing of importance turned up heare sence I rote before. brother J. M. **{Jeptha Mitchell Pittman}** was brought home and at the time I rote wee expected to bring him. Thare was none of the Stitts went to sea him buried but William. An **{Ann Stitt Pittman, Jeptha's wife}** never went. He was buried at our old place.

I have sold Mary and her child to Ben Faulkner for his land. I gave him two thousan dollars to boot for five hundred and sixty

acors of land on the Tallapoocy river. Wee
have not drawd ritings yet but I thinke he will
not backe out. I thinke I have made a very
farc trade. I thinke the land is worth eight
thousan dollars.

If you get the chance to come home you had
better come by Julafinna if the bridge is not
washed away. Wee have had the biggest freek
heare I ever saw in this countrey. The crceke
was the foolest I ever saw it. It washt away a
heep of fence and land two. Nearley all of the
mills that I have heard from is broke.

I thinke it is a bad chance to get any of the
boys to come to your company. I thinke that
tha will not go to the war till tha are made. I
thinke the boys that is seventeen will have to
go to the serve before long, but tha have all
got under seventeen.

T. S. has rented the Pollard place and movd
his family out thare. I thinke P. O. will move
to Heard on Hilabehather. I will try and
ingage your leather. Martin says make good
soldier. He. expects to join you after he gos to
school this year.

Jef Davis **{Jefferson Davis Pittman, James'
4-yr-old brother}** says if you will come
home (he) will give you the biges yam in the
hill.

I must come to a close. Rite evry opportunity
and I will do the same. We have done nothing
yet towards starting to make a crop. The

weather is so bad that wee can not worke. The collards is all kild. Wheat is vary small. I have kild all the hogs but the six little ones. Tha all was much better than I expected. One of the Eely hogs wade 215 lbs.

W. A. Pitman

Sarah Sophronia "Fronie" Davis
Child of Joshua Davis
Grandchild of William Henry Davis
July 10, 1830 – DOB
May 12, 1904 – DOD

Sarah Sophronia Davis was the daughter of Joshua Davis. Sarah was born in 1830 in Georgia. On October 10, 1854, Sarah married John Monroe Lipham. John Monroe was born in 1830 and died in 1908.

Per records, Sarah and John had the following children: William Franklin, Martha Sarah Etta "Sallie", Emma Jane "Jennie", Mary Saphronia "Babe", Charles Wilson, C. Polina Thompson "Tommie", Ada, Ida and Belle Lipham.

• **From Clarice Cox's Book LIPHAMS-OLD, YOUNG AND INBETWEEN, 1987, pp. 27-28:**
Born in Troup County, GA in 1830, John Monroe Lipham and his family moved to Heard County, GA sometime before 1850. Here he married Sarah Saphronia Davis in 1854. "Aunt Fronie," as she was called, was the youngest daughter of Joshua and Martha (Patsy) Trammel Davis, who

moved to Heard County from Wilkes County, GA before 1830.

John Monroe and Fronie lived in Heard county for several years after their marriage. According to census records, their first four children were born there. Around 1863-64 they moved over into the Taylor's Crossroad community in Randolph County, Alabama, where the remainders to their children were born. Around 1875 they moved to a farm on the Big Tallapoosa River, a few miles north of Tallapoosa, GA.

John Monroe was a prosperous farmer and businessman. He maintained a nice country home for his family and they lived well. At one time he hired a tutor to come out from Atlanta and live with the family and tutor his twin daughters, Ada and Ida. His youngest, Belle, graduated from the good graded school in Tallapoosa before 1900.

Aunt Fronie was very industrious, having inherited some of her "get up and go" from her mother "Patsy" Trammell Davis, who was said to be very industrious lady. Fronie had a loom house where she spun and wove many things necessary for the family's welfare such as jeans (a wool material) from which the men's and boys' pants were made, as well as skirts for the womenfolk. She also spun and wove cloth for other clothing and the making of quilts. Most of this material was dyed with berries and different kinds of bark from trees, roots and shrubs. As her children married, they were each given a number of the woolen coverlets (tradition says twelve), plus several cotton counterpanes, all of which were the fruits of her labor. Some of these "masterpieces" are still in the family today and are treasured by her descendants.

As soon as the older children became large enough according to John and Fronie, they were assigned a younger sibling to care for. This way Fronie was able to keep up with her weaving and other chores. I have heard my grandmother, Mary Lipham Treadway, tell of having to quit school when she was 10 and in the fourth reader, to take care of one of the twins {**Ada and Ida**}. Her older sister, Emma Jane {**Aunt Jennie]** was responsible for the care of the other. She also told of their having to milk cows as these ages, and at one time when they were caring for the twins and milking, a cow managed to get one of the twins on her crooked horns and was tossing her about before she could be rescued. Although Mary never went back to school, she was good at writing and her spelling was almost perfect.

In 1887, John Monroe and Fronie lost their home to fire and were able to save only a few of their household goods. A nice house for the times was soon erected at about the same place. My mother recalled that this was a very pretty place with bannistered porches and gingerbread trim, furnished with nice furniture - velvet platform rockers and sofas in the parlor. Fronie loved flowers and her yard was attractive and filled with boxwoods and a variety of shrubs.

About 1900 and at age 70, her health began to fail. Farm life was too much for her. It was then that she and John Monroe moved to Tallapoosa, for by this time he had an established mercantile business and held quite a bit of property. The Liphams were strong supporters of Bethany Baptist Church, which was close to their farm near Tallapoosa. Fronie moved her membership from New Hope Baptist Church in Heard County soon after moving to Haralson County, and remained a member at Bethany for the rest of her life.

Fronie died at her home in Tallapoosa May 12, 1904 after a long illness and was interred in the cemetery at Bethany. John Monroe died in his sleep at his home January 19, 1908. He sleeps in the cemetery at Bethany, also, beside his beloved "Fronie."

Letter from Ada Lipham Brock to her sisters Mary (Babe) Lipham Treadaway and Ida Lipham Brock, both in

Winnsboro, Texas: (Written on black-edged stationery, the letter was found in the trunk of Mary Lipham Treadaway after her death in 1960. All these ladies were aunts to Hettie Lipham Downs.)

Tallapoosa, Georgia
May 14, 1904 – Saturday Evening

Dear Babe and Ida:

I know you will want to hear all about the death of our dear mother Saphronia Davis Lipham, so I'll try to tell you the nearest I know. Two weeks ago last Monday, she took a bad cough and never seemed to enjoy anything to eat after that or to notice anyone. We put milk or soup in her mouth each meal and she would swallow it but we could tell she did not want it.....

She died twenty minutes before six Thursday morning. Her breathing had got easy but short about 4 o'clock. I know I never had anything so hard to bear as to see her suffer so. Belle went after Mrs. Gill when she got so bad about seven o'clock, the night before she died. She came and stayed a few minutes and stepped out and said she would be back in a few minutes. She went after Mrs.

Joe Little and old Mrs. Murdock. Before long I stepped after some cool water for Ma and Mrs. M. followed me and said for us to send after somebody else for she was already sick, and it would make her sicker to set up. I told her that I could not leave a dying mother to go for anybody.

We were left by ourselves about 4 o'clock, Bob, Belle and I. Bob (Tuggle, brother in law) had gone after (brother) Charles late the evening before, but Fannie was afraid to stay by herself and Charles did not get here until about eight the next morning. Mrs. Carroll Cobb, Mrs. Gill, Mrs. Bentley and Mrs. Smith shrouded her.

The house was full all day and so many expressed themselves as being sorry they did not know she was worse so they could have been with us. Sallie (Lipham Pittman, Saphronia's daughter), Charlotte and Loyd (Lipham, Saphronia's grandson) came that day and Hettie and the enxt day. Pa wanted Rev. Roop to preach the funeral but he could not come. Mr Jackson preached the funeral in Bethany Church at 11:30 o'clock in the presence of a large congregation. His text was "Well done thy faithful servant". Songs were "Asleep in Jesus" and "Old Time Religion". Mr. Jackson certainly made a pretty talk, and I can truthfully say he never exaggerated one bit. She had the most flowers and the prettiest ones I ever saw. More than would stay on the coffin and lots on the floor under the coffin. Ma looked more natural than she did while living. Had a pleasant sweet look and looked that way when she was buried. She was put away in a heavy, pretty black broadcloth coffin.

Surely it will most kill us to give her up and to see Pa so broken hearted. He is most killed. He wants to get right where she lay and died and takes on all the time. Last night he dreamed something and jumped off the bed, against the baby's iron bed and hurt himself pretty bad. Bruised his head and cut a right deep gash just over one eye and bruised his right hand. He was sick at his stomach for a while and his nose bled but is some better, today. He has been wanting to go to the grave all day. Belle went with him since dinner. He is worse with that nervousness and sometimes shakes all over. I fear he will not be with us long.

I am glad to my heart that I came here in the house with them. I know she had good attention during her last days and in her dying hours. All I regret is not staying during the winter. Belle gave her good attention, I know, and I found her in better condition than when I left Christmas, but I could have been with her, and now how hard it is to know that we can never see her in this life again.

Write comforting letters to Pa if you can. He is heartbroken, says he wants to stay by the grave most of his time until he can be laid by her side. He says people may think he is foolish, but he can't help it. Oscar (Ada's husband) was gone to Anniston to stand for license, when she died, but came back that night and attended the funeral.

Velma (Ida's daughter), you did not know the love for your Grandmother like poor little Thelma (Ada's daughter), and it did not hurt you to give her up. I know that we should be submissive and knowing she was a sufferer for a long time and believing she never could be well again, it seems we are doing wrong to grieve so, but our hearts are most broken and it seems that nothing can comfort us. I was so sorry for poor Pa. Such trouble at his age and in declining health. I shall never forget Mrs. Thompson and Mrs. Cobb's kindness, and others, but especially these......Your sister, Ada Brock.

May 1904 , Tallapoosa, Haralson Co, GA
- **Obituary of Sarah S. Lipham, from Tallapoosa Journal, May 1904**

We are called to mourn the passing away of another of God's pilgrims. After a long period of suffering, Mrs. Sarah S. Lipham went at the Lord's invitation to be with Jesus. There the music is sweeter and the flowers more fragrant, than the music and flowers which she was, while here, so fond of. For more than a quarter of a century she has been a devoted member of the earthly church at Bethany, but now has transferred her membership to the church of the first born, whose names are registered in Heaven.

Mrs. Sarah Lipham was affectionate to her family and kin, and never for an instant were their needs, or even their desires, unheeded. She was at all times helpful and sympathetic, wise in advice, and generous to a degree that knew no limit, save that which it was not possible to go. To the ambition of her children, she was ever responsive, encouraging them in every way that her experience and material sympathy could suggest. Her husband and children during her months of patient suffering were to her an unfailing support, never knowing weariness or impatience. Other loved ones, too, like guardian angels, succored her until the final separation came. Our sister passed away in the sunshine of her Heavenly Father's smile. Our heartfelt sympathy is extended to the family. "To be absent from the family is to be present with the Lord."

Mrs. Sarah S. Lipham was born in Franklin, Heard County, GA, on the 10th of July 1830, being at the time of her death - 5:40 a.m., May 12, 1904 - 73 years, 10 months and 2 days old. She joined the church as New Hope, Heard County, GA at about the age of 22 years. On October 12, 1854, she was married to John M. Lipham. She was the mother of two sons, W. F. Lipham, deceased, and Chas. W. Lipham, Tallapoosa, GA; also seven daughters, namely: Mrs. A. A. Pitman, Walthrall, GA; Mrs. J. R. Driver, Dallas, Texas; Mrs. Mary Treadaway, Winnsboro, Texas; Mrs. John W. Harris, deceased; Mrs. T.

W. Brock, Winnsboro, Texas; Mrs. O. H. Brock, and Mrs. R. J. Tuggle of Tallapoosa.

1895
John Monroe Lipham and wife
Sarah Sophronia "Fronie" Davis

Sarah Sophronia "Fronie" Davis Lipham

1905 John Monroe Lipham Family

Patriarch John Monroe Lipham is on top row, center. A family photograph of about 1905 depicts John Monroe Lipham as balding, with fluffy white hair and a full white beard and moustache. He appears of moderate size, neither fat nor thin, with deep-set eyes and heavy white brows. He sits on a chair placed on the front steps of his home, surrounded by 21 family members and the dog "Spot". His beloved Fronie had died in 1904.

1906 John Monroe Lipham and grandson John Robert Tuggle

Graves of John Monroe Lipham and Sarah Saphronia Davis Lipham, Bethany Baptist Church, Tallapoosa, Georgia

Wilson Lumpkin "Lummie" Davis
Child of Joshua Davis
Grandchild of William Henry Davis
December 12, 1833 – DOB
April 14, 1914 – DOD

Wilson Lumpkin Davis was the son of Joshua Davis. Wilson was born in 1833 in Heard County, Georgia. On September 9, 1855, Wilson married Emily Frances Lipham. Emily was born in 1836 and died in 1902.

Per records, Wilson and Emily had the following children: William John, Lewis Franklin III, Martha Emily, Martha Ann, Sarah Matilda, Mary Emiline (Mollie), Ella Saphronia, Dora Elizabeth, Amanda Frances and Charlie Martin Davis.

Wilson Lumpkin Davis died in 1914 in Pike City, Arkansas.

Wilson Lumpkin Davis - 1895

**1895 – Wilson Lumpkin Davis
and wife Emily Frances Lipham**

**Wilson Lumpkin Davis
Hicks Cemetery, Pike County,
Arkansas**

Richard Bines Davis
Child of Samuel Davis
Grandchild of William Henry Davis
June 15, 1817 – DOB
May 26, 1891 – DOD

Richard Bines Davis was the son of Samuel Davis. Richard was born in 1817 in Bulloch, Georgia. In March of 1860, Richard married Mary Ann Parker. Mary Ann was born in 1836 and died in 1919.

Per records, Richard and Mary Ann had the following children: Elizabeth, James Madison, Richard Andrew, George Washington, Sim Madison, Charlie, Francis J. and Mattie Davis.

Richard died in 1891 in Axson, Atkinson, Georgia.

Caroline Amelia Davis
Child of Lewis Lanier Davis
Grandchild of William Henry Davis
February 28, 1819 – DOB
February 19, 1899 – DOD

Caroline Amelia Davis was the daughter of Lewis Lanier Davis. Caroline was born in 1819 in Wilkes County, Georgia. On October 28, 1834, Caroline married Sanders Walker Faver in Wilkes County, Georgia. Sanders was born in 1808 and died in 1881.

Per records, Caroline and Sanders had the following children: John Thomas, Louisa Ann, William Allen, Teresa, Lurissa, Mary Elizabeth "Lizzie", Hariet Isabella, Lewis Davis, Isaiah Tucker, Sanders Walker and Cora Alice Faver.

Caroline Amelia died in 1899 in Heard County, Georgia.

Caroline Amelia Davis

Ann Cordella Davis
Child of Lewis Lanier Davis
Grandchild of William Henry Davis
1820 – DOB – Wilkes County Georgia
1872 – DOD – Coweta County Georgia

Ann Cordella was the daughter of Lewis Lanier Davis. Ann married Tolbert Xenithon Reese. Xenithon was born in 1816 and died in 1859.

Per records, Ann and Xenithon had one child by the name of William Irvin Reese.

Ann Cordella died in 1872 in Coweta County, Georgia.

Isaiah Tucker Davis
Child of Lewis Lanier Davis
Grandchild of William Henry
Davis
1822 – DOB

William L. Davis
Child of Lewis Lanier Davis
Grandchild of William Henry
Davis
1824 – DOB

Andrew J. Davis
Child of Lewis Lanier Davis
Grandchild of William Henry
Davis
1826 – DOB

Isabella Davis
Child of Lewis Lanier Davis
Grandchild of William Henry
Davis
1828 – DOB – Wilkes County,
Georgia

Nancy Davis
Child of Lewis Lanier Davis
Grandchild of William Henry Davis
1829 – DOB – Wilkes County, Georgia

Splinters = Great Grandchildren of Lieutenant Colonel William Henry Davis

277 Great Grandchildren Recorded

Emily Davis 1826-1886
Nancy Davis 1828-1879
Margaret Livador Davis 1829-1903
Elizabeth Davis – 1830-1835
Edward Davis 1831-1912 – (STORY BELOW)
Jane Davis 1834-1866
Samuel Webster Davis 1836-1905 (STORY BELOW)
Franklin M. Davis 1838-1870
Martha A. Davis 1840-1919
Presley Davis 1841-1863
William Marshall Davis 1844-1910
Sarah Lucinda Davis 1850-1914
William P. Davis 1824-1859
Wylanty P. Davis 1828-1880
Narcissa Malinda Davis 1830-1925
Hezakiah Kirah Davis 1851-1876 (STORY BELOW)
Amberson Davis 1853-1870
Celestia Lisa Davis 1855-1910

Alfred Davis
Ansley Davis
Isaiah Davis
James Davis
Lavina E. Davis 1825-1865
Mary Gresham Davis 1800-1850
Harriett L. Davis 1813
Edward Davis 1822-1869
Joshua LT Davis 1823-1867
John Martin Davis 1825-1901
Judith Agnes Davis 1826-1872
William B. Davis 1828-1866
Elizabeth Jane Davis 1830-1906
(STORY BELOW)
Dr. Elias Davis 1833-1864
Ralph Davis 1836-1895
Lanie Ann Davis 1839
Amanda Davis 1840
Edward Lee Davis 1843-1866
Mary B. Davis 1844
Mellissa Davis 1849
Fereby Davis
Mary Davis
Nancy Davis
William Davis
James Franklin Davis 1832-1894
(STORY BELOW)
Missouri Davis 1836
Malissa/Marisa Davis 1839
Lila Ann (Zilly Ann) Davis 1840
Margaret Ann Davis 1842-1924

Amanda Davis 1844-1920
Mary Elizabeth Davis 1847
Tennessee Davis 1852
Augustus C. Davis 1855
William B. McLeod 1843-1922
Susan McLeod 1844-1912
Zillian Ann McLeod 1847-1925
Caroline Saline McLeod 1847-1919
Sara Jane McLeod 1847-1932
Morgan M. McLeod 1848-1918
(STORY BELOW)
Frances McLeod 1852-1925
Sarah Jane Davis 1840-1910
Susan A. Davis 1842-1916
Mary Evelyn "Emily" Davis 1844
Amanda Davis 1848
Clara F. Davis 1850
James Davis Jr. 1853-1930
Allen Davis 1855-1908
Yancey Davis 1861-1919
Thomas Walter Overton 1840-1880
John F. Overton 1845
James E. Overton 1847
Sarah R. Overton 1856
Lizzy R. Overton 1857
Martha G. Overton 1859
Edward Davis Grumbles 1846-1881
Harriet Elizabeth Grumbles 1847-
1903
Margaret Keziah Grumbles 1849

Winnifred Armita Grumbles 1850-
1915
William Henry Grumbles 1851-1874
Martha Ann Grumbles 1853-1941
Mary Jane Grumbles 1855-1938
Susan Caroline (Carrie) Grumbles
1857-1932
Louisa Ann (Ludy) Grumbles 1859-
1922
Benjamin Franklin Grumbles 1862
Charles Glover Grumbles 1864-1931
Thomas Green Grumbles 1866-1880
Sarah Mellisa Grumbles 1869-1873
William Franklin Davis 1866-1944
John Noble Davis 1868-1956
(STORY BELOW)
Nancy Avarillah Davis 1870-1938
Thomas Mark Davis 1871-1935
Reuben Marshall Davis 1874-1940
Robert Shelton Davis 1877-1938
Jerry Lee Davis 1881-1906
Mary Cryssa Davis 1882-1978
(STORY BELOW)
Arthur Robertson Davis 1884-1970
Ardelia May "Delia" Davis 1887-
1919 (STORY)
Sarah Alta Davis 1891-1908
Reuben Bennett Jr. 1813
Thomas Bennett 1815
Mary Elizabeth Bennett 1816
Harvey Davis 1816

Elizabeth Davis 1818-1892
Nancy Davis 1820
Mary Davis 1822
Samantha Agnes Davis 1824-1861
William Edwin Davis 1827-1904
Thomas L. Davis 1830-1863
Martha F. Davis 1833-1860
Mariah Davis 1835
James H. Davis 1838-1860
William Thomas Davis 1828-1907
James S. Davis 1829-1860
Mary Ann Elizabeth Davis 1830-1889
Jacob Emmissy Davis 1832-1865
John R. Davis 1835-1907
Joseph Julius Davis 1838-1874
Sarah Agnes Davis 1844-1905
Benjamin Franklin Davis 1847-1900
William Davis Beck 1825-1871
(STORY BELOW)
John Thomas Beck 1827-1903
(STORY BELOW)
Joshua Emasy Beck 1829-1901
(STORY BELOW)
Mary Frances Beck 1833-1838
Fredonia Ann Beck 1836-1862
(STORY BELOW)
Darthula Mary Frances Beck 1838-
1864
Judge Beck 1841-1842
Morning C. Beck 1841-1884
Orrin Alston Jr. Beck 1842-1875

James Owen Beck 1845-1919
Martha McDaniel 1830-1906
Sarah Agnes Mary Elizabeth
McDaniel 1834-1910
Thomas Marley McDaniel 1838-1887
Edwin McDaniel 1824-1846
William McDaniel 1826-1846
Samuel McDaniel 1828-1846
John T. McDaniel 1845-1846
Isaac Newton Stewart 1828-1916
Mary Ann Stewart 1832-1914
Jonathan Milton Stewart 1834-1911
Martha E. Stewart 1837
Wiley D. Stewart 1843
Charles J. Stewart 1849-1929
William Franklin Stewart 1852-1921
Joseph Wiley Stewart 1838-1862
Martha Gresham Davis 1820-1859
James Benjamin Davis 1827-1902
Henry Davis 1826-1919
John Marion Davis 1829-1898
Roxie Ann Davis 1831-1904
Adolphus Dakota Davis 1833-1862
William Calloway Davis 1837-1911
George Granberry Davis 1840-1917
(STORY)
William Gold Davis 1826
Narissa Davis 1829
Elizabeth B. Davis 1832
James W. Davis 1834-1900

George Washington Davis 1838-1917
(STORY)
Martha Jane Davis 1840-1865
Mary Amanda Davis 1845-1882
William B. Davis 1848
Thomas B. Davis 1852
Victoria B. Davis 1854
Laura Elizabeth Davis 1858
Frances Murneva Davis 1864-1941
Henry C. Davis 1868
John B. Davis 1871
Leroy Davis 1873
Joshua Davis 1875
Christopher Columbus Davis 1878-
1959
Elizabeth Jones 1828-1907
Catherine Jones 1835
Dr Charles Gresham Jones 1837-
1924
William Calloway Jones 1840-1915
Mary D. Jones 1843
Thomas Jones 1843
Harriet J. Jones 1847
Julia E. Jones 1848-1892
Benjamin J. Jones 1850-1889
Tip Jones 1854-1885
Judith Ann Hadley 1840-1933
Eleanor Ellen Hadley 1845
Joseph Davis Hadley 1851-1926
Thomas Hadley 1857
Jonas Hadley 1860

John J. Hadley 1862
Charles G. Lyle 1837-1929 (STORY
BELOW)
Elizabeth E. Lyle 1838
Mary Jane Lyle 1842-1931
James Davis "Jim" Lyle 1844-1930
(STORY)
Margaret Lyle 1846-1852
Martha Ann Lyle 1845-1929
Missouri M. Lyle 1850-1870
Berryman Erastus Lyle 1852-1936
Isabelle Eunice Lyle 1852
William Franklin Lyle 1856-1931
Richard C. Lyle 1857-1887
Judith Lyle 1860
Thomas Milton Lyle 1861-1927
Thomas S. Davis 1850
Martha Melissa Davis 1841-1908
(STORY BELOW)
Nancy Diana Davis 1842-1843
Mary Elizabeth Davis 1844-1907
(STORY BELOW)
Martin Joshua Davis 1845-1916
(STORY BELOW)
William Owen Davis 1847-1941
(STORY BELOW)
Lewis Franklin "Dock" Jr. Davis
1849-1938 (STORY BELOW)
Emily Teresa "Emma" Davis 1851-
1938

James Thadeus "Jim" Davis 1852-
1905
George Pittman Davis 1854-1867
Andrew Smith Davis 1856-1902
(STORY BELOW)
William F. Taylor 1833-1860
John B. Taylor 1835-1860
Martha Serepta Taylor 1836-1918
Oliver Taylor 1839-1865
James Paschal Taylor 1842-1860
Owen Harrison Taylor 1843-1917
Mary Ann Taylor 1846
Peter Taylor 1848-1922 (STORY
BELOW)
Shady A.J. Taylor 1849-1936
L. Thomas Davis 1846
James A. Davis 1848
Elizabeth "Lizzie" Davis 1850-1932
Baby Girl (Twin) Ridley 1844-1844
Baby Girl (Twin) Ridley 1844-1844
Saphronia Balsora Ridley 1847-1927
William Franklin Ridley 1850-1855
Warren Ales Ridley 1853-1925
Martha Ella Ridley 1856-1933
William Davis Ridley 1859-1939
Polly Smith Ridley 1862-1934
Alice Lee Ridley 1866-1921
James Franklin Pittman 1847-1922
(STORY)
Joshua Martin Pittman 1849-1918

**Martha Elizabeth "Sis" Pittman
1851-1928**
**William Alfonso Pittman Jr. 1853-
1855**
Nancy Smith "Nan" Pittman 1855-
1944 (STORY)
**William Alphonso II Pittman 1857-
1860**
William Owen Pittman 1859-1860
Jefferson Davis Pittman 1861-1947
Etta Jane Pittman 1864-1946
(STORY BELOW)
Addie Balsora Pittman 1868-1932
William Franklin Lipham 1855-1889
(STORY)
Martha Sarah Etta "Sallie" Lipham
1857-1906 (STORY BELOW)
Emma Jane "Jennie" Lipham 1859-
1946 (STORY)
Mary Saphronia "Babe" Lipham
1862-1960 (STORY BELOW)
Charles Wilson Lipham 1865-1938
(STORY)
C. Polina Thompson "Tommie"
Lipham 1868-1894 (STORY BELOW)
Ada Lipham 1872-1959 (STORY
BELOW)
Ida Lipham 1872-1961 (STORY
BELOW)
Belle Lipham 1875-1970 (STORY
BELOW)

William John Davis 1856-1930
Lewis Franklin III Davis 1859-1908
(STORY)
Martha Emily Davis 1862
Martha Ann Davis 1863
Sarah Matilda Davis 1866-1932
Mary Emiline "Mollie" Davis 1868
Ella Saphronia Davis 1871-1926
Dora Elizabeth Davis 1875-1953
Amanda Frances Davis 1878
Charlie Martin Davis 1882-1896
Elizabeth Davis 1861-1934 (STORY
BELOW)
James Madison Davis 1864-1941
Richard Andrew Davis 1866-1925
George Washington Davis 1869-1950
Sim Madison Davis 1872-1964
Charlie Davis 1874-1960
Francis J. Davis 1874-1946
Mattie Davis 1877-1927
John Thomas Faver 1835-1906
(STORY BELOW)
Louisa Ann Faver 1837-1910
(STORY BELOW)
William Allen Faver 1841-1912
Teresa Faver 1845-1928 (STORY
BELOW)
Lurissa Faver 1845
Mary Elizabeth "Lizzie" Faver 1847-
1929
Harriet Isabella Faver 1850-1885

Lewis Davis Faver 1853-1940
Isaiah Tucker Faver 1856-1878
Sanders Walker Faver 1859-1866
Cora Alice Faver 1862-1915
William Irvin Reese 1847-1926

41 Stories out of the 277 great
grandchildren listed above will be
included in this book.
More stories will be included in the
next book.

Edward Davis
Child of William Davis
Grandson of Edward and Margaret Davis
Great-Grandchild of William Henry Davis
September 11, 1831 – DOB
January 16, 1912 – DOD

EDWARD DAVIS was the son of William and Elizabeth Davis. Edward served with the Confederate 53rd Alabama Calvary (Partisan Rangers) Company B and was ranked a Private in the Army.

On January 2, 1855, Edward married Caroline Whittington in Pike County, Alabama. Caroline was born in 1829 and died in 1902. Per records, Edward and Caroline's children were Georgia Ann and Mary E. Davis. Both children were born prior to Edward being enlisted in the infantry.

The 53rd regiment of mounted infantry was organized in the fall of 1862. Edward enlisted on August 5th 1862 in Troy, Alabama under Captain Hamner during war time. Edward was 31 years old at the time of his enlistment.

The Muster Roll of 1862 states that Edward "received fifty dollars in full for my bounty." Muster Roll of May and June of

1863 has Edward listed as "absent…..about on sick furlough Chattanooga" but has him listed as present on duty by the June 30 to October 31, 1863 muster roll. Documents show where Edward Davis requested a prisoner of war record (possibly for his brother, Presley's arrest.)

Per records, Edward Davis was described as being 5 foot 11 inches tall, dark complexion with hazel eyes and dark hair.

During Edwards's elder years, he married Mary Etta McLeod who was 22 years old. Edward and Mary Etta were married on January 19, 1904. Mary Etta was born in 1882 and died in 1970. At the time of their marriage, Edward was 72 years old and Mary Etta was 22 years old.

At the time of Edwards's death, his wife received her husband's military pension. His wife continued to draw her husband's military pension until her death. Mary Etta was one of the oldest living Confederate widows to draw a war pension in the state of Alabama up until the time of her death.

Edward Davis and his first wife, Caroline, are both buried at the Davis Cemetery in Troy, Alabama.

Edward Davis
Troy, Alabama

Caroline Whittington
Davis Family Cemetery in Troy
Alabama

Davis, Edward

Co. B, **53** Alabama
(Partisan Rangers).
(Confederate.)

Private | Private

CARD NUMBERS.

Edward Davis was 30 years old at the time of his enlistment in 1862

Davis Edward

Pvt., Co. "B" 53 Reg't Ala Cav

(Confederate.)

Inclosures.

Bed Cards	Final Statements
Burial Records	Furloughs or L. of A
Certs. of Dis. for Discharge	Med. Certificates
C. M. Charges	Med. Des. Lists
Descriptive Lists	Orders
Discharge Certificates	Pris. of War Record
Enlistment Papers	Resignations

Edward Davis request for prisoner of war records

53

(Partisan Rangers.)

Ala.

2

Edward C. Davis

Pvt. { Capt. Hanner's Co., 53 Reg't
Alabama Partisan Rangers.*

Age............ years.

Appears on

Company Muster Roll

of the organization named above,

for .... *class of c* ...., 186 2.

Joined for duty and enrolled:

When ...., 186 .

Where ....

By whom ....

Period .... *the war* ....

Remarks: *Received ... fifty*
dollars in full for my
bounty

*This company subsequently became Company H 53d Regiment Alabama Partisan Rangers.

Book mark : ....

.... *Wm. Estrada* ....

(655)

Copyist.

Edward Davis 1862
"Received fifty dollars in full for my
bounty"

Confederate.

5:3

(Partisan Rangers.)

Ala.

Edward Davis

Pvt., Co. B, 53 Regiment Alabama Partisan Rangers.

Appears on

Company Muster Roll

of the organization named above,

for *Aug 5 to Sept 30*, 186 *2*

Enlisted:
When *Aug 5* , 186 *2*
Where *Troy Ala*
By whom *Capt Gardner*
Period *war*

Last paid:
By whom *Capt Dickinson*
To what time *Sept 30* , 186 *2*

Present or absent *Present*

Remarks:

Book mark:

Ala. Records

(642)

Copyist.

Muster Roll for Aug 5 to Sept. 30, 1862
Edward Davis – 30 yrs old

(Confederate.)

53
(Partisan Rangers.)

Ala.

Edward Davis

Pvt, Co. I, 53 Regiment Alabama
Partisan Rangers.

Appears on

Company Muster Roll

of the organization named above,

for _____, 1863.

Enlisted:
When _____ Aug 5 _____, 186_.
Where _____ Troy Ala _____
By whom _____ Capt Hammer _____
Period _____ war _____

Last paid:
By whom _____ Bell Dickerson _____
To what time _____ Apr 30 _____, 186_.

Present or absent _____ Absent _____
Remarks: Absent on sick furlough
Chattanooga

Book mark:

_____

(842)   Copyist.

**Muster Roll for May and June of
1863
Edward listed as absent…about on
sick furlough Chattanooga
Edward Davis – 31 yrs old**

| D | 53 Partisan Rangers | Ala |

Ed Da vis

Co. B, 53 Regt. Ala. Vols.

Appears on a
        RECEIPT ROLL

for clothing,

for............................. 1 Qr. ...., 186 4 .

Date of issue........................., 186 .
Signature   E. Davis
Remarks :..

Receipt Roll
Edward Davis 1864

Samuel Webster Davis
Child of William Davis
Grandchild of Edward and Margaret Davis
Great-Grandchild of William Henry Davis
June 13, 1836 – DOB per gravestone
June 13, 1835 – DOB per family Bible
February 6, 1905 – DOD per gravestone
February 6, 1907 – DOD per family Bible

Samuel Davis was the son of William and Elizabeth Duncan Davis. Samuel served in the War Between the States, as did his brothers Edward and Presley. They all served in the Confederate 53rd Alabama Partisan Rangers Company B Army and were all ranked Privates. Company Muster Roll shows that Samuel enlisted on August 5, 1862 in Troy, Alabama by Captain Hamner during war time.

Samuel Davis married Mary Ann Cantaline Carnley who was born on August 1, 1833 in Alabama. They were married on February 10, 1855 in Pike County, Alabama per marriage records. Samuel and Mary Ann had the following children: William Matthew

"Matt", Manday E., Sarah Katherine, Mary Emmer, Samuel Presley, Tennessee Everline, Joseph Franklin (Frank), **John Oscar** and Minnie Ola Davis.

Samuel suffered from Bright's disease. He also suffered from chronic Cystitis caused by an enlarged prostate.

Samuel and Mary Ann Carnley Davis are buried in the old Davis family cemetery which is located in Troy, Alabama in Pike County.

- Troy Messenger
Wednesday, February 15, 1905
Sam Davis dead "from Wednesdays Daily" We are informed that Sam Davis, one of the oldest and most esteemed citizens of the county, died Monday afternoon at the home of his son, Matt Davis, a few miles west of Troy. We understand that he was an ex-confederate soldier, and a member of the Primitive Baptist Church. He was a brother of William Davis. He is survived by his children. The sympathy of many friends is extended the sorrowing relatives.

Samuel Davis
Davis Family Cemetery in Troy,
Alabama

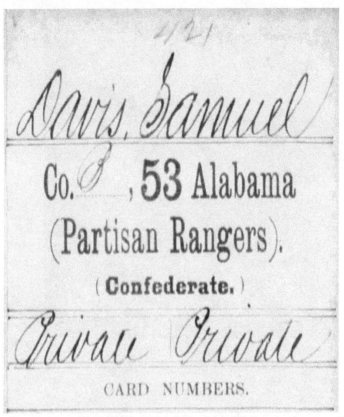

Samuel Davis was 26 yrs old at time of enlistment in 1862

Capt. Hunner's Co., 53 Reg't
Alabama Partisan Rangers.*

Age _____ years.

Appears on

Company Muster Roll

of the organization named above,

for _____, 186 2

Joined for duty and enrolled:

When _____, 186 .

Where _____

By whom _____

Period _____

Remarks: *Received fifty dollars in full for my bounty*

*This company subsequently became Company H, 53d Regiment Alabama Partisan Rangers.

Book mark: _____

(655)   Copyist.

Samuel Davis – 1862
"Received fifty dollars in full for
my bounty"

53
(Partisan Rangers.)
Ala.

Samuel Davis

Pvt., Co. 3 } 53 Regiment Alabama
Partisan Rangers.

Appears on

Company Muster Roll

of the organization named above,

for *Aug 5 to Sept 3*, 186 2.

Enlisted :
When *Aug. 5* , 186 2
Where *Tuscaloosa*
By whom *Lieut. Alexander*
Period *war*

Last paid:
By whom *Capt Dickinson*
To what time *Sept 30*, 186 2.

Present or absent *Present*

Remarks :

Book mark :

M. Lucas

(642) Copyist.

**Muster Roll from Aug 5 to Sept30,
1862
Samuel Davis – 26 yrs old**

53

(Partisan Rangers.) | **Ala.**

_____ _____ ___

P_b , Co. D } 53 Regiment Alabama
Partisan Rangers.

Appears on

Company Muster Roll

of the organization named above,

for _May & June_ , 186 3 .

Enlisted :

When _____ , 186 .

Where _____

By whom _____

Period ____

Last paid :

By whom _____

To what time _____ , 186 .

Present or absent _____

Remarks :

Book mark :

_____

(642) Copyist.

Muster Roll for May and June of 1863
Samuel Davis – 27 yrs old

D | 53 Partisan Rangers | Ala

Saml. Davis

Co. B, 53 Regt. Ala. Vols.

Appears on a

RECEIPT ROLL

for clothing,

for .... 1 Qr. ......, 186 4 .

Date of issue ...., 186 .
Signature   Samuel Davis
Remarks: ....

Receipt Roll – 1864
Samuel Davis – 28 yrs old

Hezakiah (Kirah) Davis
Child of Isaac B. Davis
Grandchild of Edward Davis
Great-Grandchild of William Henry Davis
1851 – DOD
June 16, 1876 – DOD

Hezakiah Davis was the son of Isaac B. Davis. Hezakiah was born in 1851 in Jefferson County, Georgia. On December 30, 1868, Hezakiah married Ellen Eliza Ponder in Jefferson County, Georgia. Ellen was born in 1848 and died in 1914.

Per records, Hezakiah and Ellen had the following children: Ephriam J. and William John Davis.

Hezakiah (Kirah) Davis died in 1876 after shooting himself and by overdosing on Iodnum (Iodine). He died in Burke, Georgia.

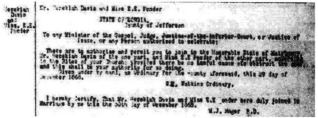

Marriage Certificate of Hezakiah Davis and Ellen Eliza Ponder
December 30, 1868

Elizabeth Jane Davis
Child of Dr. Daniel Davis
Grandchild of Edward Davis
Great-Grandchild of William Henry Davis
May 1830 – DOB
1906 – DOD

Elizabeth Jane Davis was the daughter of Dr. Daniel Davis. Elizabeth was born in 1830 in Tuscaloosa, Alabama. In 1853, Elizabeth married George William Marshall. George was born in 1828 and died in 1904.

Per records, Elizabeth and George had the following children: Margaret Elizabeth, Mary A., Ida Bell, Elizabeth Bettie, Rose E., Rosa, Katie and Catherine Marshall.

Elizabeth Jane Davis Marshall died in 1906 in Birmingham, Alabama.

Elizabeth Jane Davis Marshall
James Franklin Davis
Child of Presley Davis
Grandchild of Edward Davis
Great-Grandchild of William Henry Davis
December 18, 1832 – DOB
April 5, 1894 – DOD

James Franklin Davis was the son of Presley Davis. James was born in 1832 in Lowndes County, Alabama.

On October 2, 1851, James Franklin married Martha Ann Grainger. Martha was born in 1835 and died in 1870. Per records, James Franklin and Martha Ann had the following children: William Franklin, Augustus C., Mary P., Frances Rebecca, John Presley and Malissa Davis.

On July 16, 1871, James Franklin married Dicey Jane Dempsey in Lafayette Arkansas. Dicey Jane was born in 1842 and died in 1887. Per records, James Franklin and Dicey Jane had the following children: Marie Etta and Jessie Howard Davis.

Records show that James Franklin's last marriage was to Sarah Elizabeth Ragsdale on July 24, 1888. Sarah was born in 1842 and died in 1930.

James Franklin Davis died in 1894.
He is buried at Macedonia Baptist Church
Cemetery in Miller County, Arkansas.

- Will of James Franklin Davis
Know all men by these present:
That I James F. Davis of the county of
Miller and State of Arkansas being in ill
health but of sound and disposing mind
and memory do make and publish this my
last will and testament hereby revoking
all former wills by me at any time
heretofore made;
1st - I hereby constitute and appoint my
son William F. Davis to be the sole
executor of my last will directing my said
executor to pay all my just debts and
funeral expenses and the legacies herein
after given out of my estate.
2nd - After the payments of my said
debts and funeral expenses I give my
wife Mrs Sarah E Davis one burrau that
she is now using. And to my son William
one feather bed and the other bedding
that belongs theirto.
3rd - I give and bequeth to my son Jesse
H. Davis, three hundred dollars in cash
seperate from his other part of his share
in my estate to be held by my executor
until he becomes of the age of fifteen or

sixteen years and then to be used for the purpose of educating him if his guardian thinks it advisable and that his brother William becomes his guardian until he becomes of age if death does not interfear.

4th - I devise that my executor take the residue of all the rest of my estate both real and personal in charge and proceed to sell the same as soon after my burial as he thinks advisable and divide the proceeds as the same equally between my legal and lawful heirs.

5th - I request and advise that if the law and heirs will admit that my executor this will without Bond, but if he cannot, according to law that he executes the Same, any Way as the law directs.

6th - I devise that my son Jesse have one feather twin bed only that belongs thereto, and also one zink trunk that is his own property and I further devise that my daughter Marie E. Davis has one Feather Bed and all bedding that belongs thereto also one Trunk and on Marble top Bureau before there is any sale or division made of my property.

7th - I also devise that my wife Sarah E. Davis has all of her house hold furniture

consisting of 2 feather beds and bedding thereto belonging and other house hold and kitchen furniture that she had when me and her were married for and remain her separate property. And I further devise that any property that she may have during life from my Estate at her death be divided equally among my heirs. In testamony where of I hereunto set my hand and publish and declare this to be my last will and testament on the punsince of the witness nowed below this 18th day of September A.D.
1892 ....James F. Davis
Signed published and declared by the said James F. Davis as and for his last will and testament in presants of us who in his presants and in teh presants of each other and at his request have subscribed our names as witnesses hereto: Geo. L. Bell, Wesley E. Patillo. Filed 11 June 1894 and admitted to Probate 3 July 1894, J.V. Scott, Clerk.

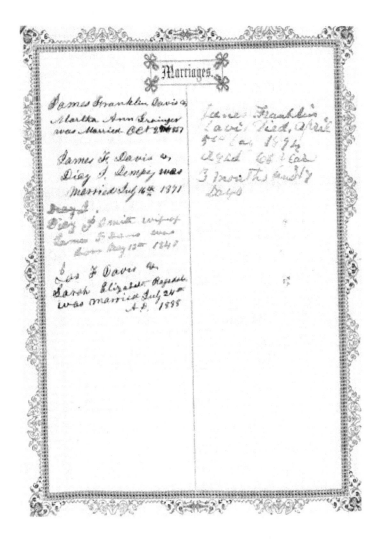

Page from Family Bible
James Franklin Davis

Morgan M. McLeod
Child of Mary Polly Davis
Grandchild of Edward Davis
Great-Grandchild of William Henry Davis
January 2, 1848 – DOB
October 20, 1918 – DOD

Morgan M. McLeod was the son of Morgan McLeod. Morgan was born in 1848 in Pike County, Alabama. On January 28, 1875, Morgan married Susan Adeline Kelly in Pike County, Alabama. Susan was born in 1857 and died in 1931.

Per records, Morgan and Susan had the following children: Emma Doris, Charles Franklin, Ollie Washington, Ida Bell, Joseph Bryant, Alexander and John Daniel McLeod.

Morgan M. McLeod died in 1918. Morgan is buried at Oak Grove Cemetery.

- story written by Morgan's granddaughter/ Patsye Ruth Harris Lucas

- Morgan and Susan settled on the rich, flat lands near where Beaman Creek runs into Conecuh River. Morgan's parents, Mary Davis and Bryant, lived across the river in another community about four miles west of Troy on what is now called the Shellhorn Road. Their land was a farm that bordered the river. It is thought that Morgan's and his parents land lines met in the Conecuh swamp area.

Morgan and Susan began married life in a log and plank house sitting at the edge of a large field. Later around 1908 Morgan built Susan a larger home up on the Oak Grove Raod close to the first home. It had six rooms with a wide hall. The front porch extended all across the front. The back porch extended from the end of the hall to as long as two rooms. The last room at the end of the porch was the kitchen. The kitchen always smelled of coffee, biscuits, honey and some kind of meat being fried. Morgan painted the home an antique green and trimmed it in white. The front door was wide and heavy with on half being glass.

Morgan, son of Mary Davis, was a quiet, gentle person who was soft spoken and kind. He never got in a hurry. He had dark curly hair, olive complexion and dark brown eyes. He was a medium stature. Two of his children, Ida Bell and

Charles Franklin inherited his markings. Two of Ida Bell's children, Margaret Sydney and Roy Edmundson also inherited Morgan's looks.

Morgan was a member of the Mt. Gilliard Primitive Baptist Church. Once a month he walked from his farm to his church which was located on the Harmony Road on the old 231 Montgomery highway. The ancient cemetery is still there where many of his relatives were buried.

One year Morgan and his wife, Susan Adeline Kelly, made a good crop and after debts were paid, cleared fifty dollars. Morgan went to Troy on his buggy and among other things, purchased a brand new shot gun. Needless to say Susan was upset for she figured they needed something else, for instance, land. One year the farm next door became available to buy. It was the Parker place. Susan said "Morg, let's buy the land. Morg replied, "We can't we're not able right now" That night Susan secretly went outside somewhere and dug up some gold pieces that she had buried in a jar. The next day she handed the gold to Morgan, and he went and purchased the land. The land is still owned by Morgan's grandchildren.

In his last days Morgan developed heart dropsy. His legs swelled. Little broken places appeared and water ran down his legs. He walked slowly and haltingly. Every day he tried to walk down the road to his youngest son's home, and return by roads throught the cotton and corn fields. He liked to watch his flocks of geese and guinea scurring through the fields eating insects and seeds. He especially loved his first two grandsons, Fred Lyons and Roy Edmundson Harris. Both boys were mean and spoiled. Fred cried wo when his aunt Ida Bell married that Grandmaw Susan made Ida Bell and her new husband, John Wilson Harris, take him along on their honeymoon to Montgomery. John never forgave Fred. No one could ever do anything with Morgan's grandson, Roy. He was trying to walk at seven months. One day when he was less than two years old he climbed, by some unknown means, on top of Morgan's house. Morgan nearly had a heart attack. Finally he coaxed, after begging and pleading, Roy, to back down a ladder that he hastily been built.

Morgan McLeod died in the year 1918, in the fall. During his sickness he had lain on a cot out in the wide hall of his home so a breeze could be felt. He had lain there all summer. On his burial day Woods Funeral Home sent out a black herse drawn by two strong horses. They backed it up to the rail fence in front. Then friends carried the body to the hearse. The family followed in buggies, wagons, and walking. They didn'ts have to go far, just around two sharp curves and there was the church. Morgan used to sit on his front porch, and look across Lee's big field and there was the church and cemetery. They laid him to rest by his oldest daughter, Emma McLeod Lyons, who had died earlier of tuberculosis. A thick marble slab, with his name and a beautiful marble vase was placed on his grave.

After Morgan's death, Susan became the strong one to lead the family and to hold the farm together. 1918 had been a hard year on everyone. The terrible influenza epidemic occurred when so many people died. Morgan's son, Charles Franklin, had the ailment, andhe never completely overed it.

Years before, around 1866, Morgan's father, Bryant McLeod 1812-1866 died leaving Mary Davis and her children. The Civil War had just ended. The oldest son, William, had gone to war. Upon returning he tried to take over the estate. A long law suit followed. Finally it ended. Morgan's sibblings, William, Jane Frances and Zillie Ann went to live in lower Montgomery County. Morgan married and moved to Oak Grove. Some of his sisters lived with him after their Mother either died or was killed in Conecuh Swamp. She had been walking from her home to Oak Grove to see her sick relative. She never arrived. Her mangled body was later found. There was a rift in the Mary Davis family aftger the law suit. It was never talked, but descendants wondered why there was no visiting.

It is gratifying to know that Morgan was always close and helpful to his Mother, Mary Davis, formally of Dallas County, Alabama, Wilks County, Georgia and born somewhere in South Carolina.

Susan Adeline Kelly McLeod 1852-1931
Morgan M. McLeod 1849-1918
Child: Either Bryant McLeod or Fred Lyons

B. S. MATTOCKS,   Troy, Ala.

Grand parents of Patsye Ruth Harris Lucas 1925

John Noble Davis
Child of John Henry Davis
Grandchild of Edward Davis
Great-Grandchild of William Henry Davis
April 10, 1868 – DOB
February 2, 1956 – DOD

John Noble Davis was the son of John Henry Davis. John Noble was born in 1868 in Hays, Texas.

In 1889, John Noble married Martha Ann "Mattie" Lumbley. Martha was born in 1865 and died in 1900. Per records, John Noble and Martha Ann had the following children: William "Willie", Nancy Catherine "Kate" and Joe Dee "Jodie" Davis.

On February 15, 1903, John Noble married Ella Eudora Almand. Ella was born in 1879 and died in 1956. Per records, John Noble and Ella had the following children: Lillie Estella, Laura Francis, Elmer Lonnie, Marie "Pinkie" and Gladys Elizabeth Davis.

John Noble Davis died in 1956 in Gorman, Eastland, Texas. John Noble is buried at DeLeon City Cemetery in DeLeon, Comanche, Texas.

**John Noble and Martha Ann Davis
1891**

John Noble Davis
1891

Smallest child—Joe Dee Davis, Bill "Willie" Davis, John Noble Davis and Nancy Catherine "Kate" Davis

Ella Eudora Almand Davis and John Noble Davis

**Home of John Noble Davis
1956 – Gorman, Eastland, Texas**

John Noble Davis

**John Noble Davis
DeLeon City Cemetery in DeLeon,
Comanche, Texas**

Mary Cryssa "Crissie" Davis
Child of John Henry Davis
Grandchild of Edward Davis
Great-Grandchild of William Henry
Davis
October 13, 1882 – DOB
December 29, 1978 – DOD

Mary Cryssa "Crissie" Davis
was the daughter of John Henry Davis.
Crissie was born in 1882 in Texas.

On July 19, 1904, Mary Cryssa married
Theodore Carrie "Corry" Marshall. Theodore
was born in 1880 and died in 1963.

Per records, Mary Cryssa and Theodore
had the following children: Lois Gladys,
Nettie Opal, Oscar, Lonnie Paul, Oleta Lou,
Corrie Lea and Troy Rufus Marshall.

Mary Cryssa Davis Marshall died in
1978 in Cisco, Eastland, Texas.

Mary Crissie Davis and Ardelia May Davis

Mary Cryssa Davis
1902 – 20 years old

Mary Cryssa and Theodore
Carrie Marshall

Edgar Marshall, Theodore "Corry" Marshall, Mary Cryssa Davis Marshall 1947

THEADORE CORRY
MARSHALL
JUNE 10. 1880
APRIL 29. 1963

Ardelia May "Delia" Davis
Child of John Henry Davis
Grandchild of Edward Davis
Great-Grandchild of William Henry Davis
May 26, 1887 – DOB
August 18, 1919 – DOD

Ardelia May "Delia" Davis was the daughter of John Henry Davis. Ardelia was born in 1887 in Llano (Indian Creek) Texas.

On October 29, 1908, Ardelia married Christopher Colombus "Lum" Marlin in Brownwood, Texas. Christopher was born in 1886 and died in 1919.

Per records, Ardelia and Christopher had the following children: Christopher Colombus Jr. and his twin died in infancy, Leonard Stephens and Grace Irene "Gracie" Marlin.

Ardelia's husband, Christopher, died in the influenza epidemic of 1918. He was sick for three days before his death. On his death certificate, his cause of death was "acute Nephritis with pneumonia." Christopher was a smoker and a drinker.

Ardelia was heart broken over the death of her husband. Ardelia would cry for days on end and refused to eat. It is believed that she died emotionally from a broken heart and physically from "consumption" or tuberculosis.

Nancy Avarillah, Ardelia's older sister, raised Ardelia's two young children, Leonard and Grace Marlin.

Ardelia May "Delia" Davis Marlin died in 1919 in Lohn, McCullough, Texas.

Obituary for Ardelia May Davis Marlin

Brady (Mason), Texas, USA –Friday, August 22, 1919

Mrs. Marlin died Friday at E.A. Marshall home in Lohn, Texas, August 18, 1919. We are sorry to report the death of Mrs. Marlin, who has been very sick for several months.   She passed quietly away last Friday night at the home of her sister, Mrs. E.A. Marshall. She leaves two small children, a boy and a girl, who will make their home with Mrs. Marshall.   At the time of her death, Mrs. Marlin was 33 years of age. The sympathy of all goes to Mrs. Marshall for the loss of her sister. Mrs. Davis, who was called here on account of her daughter's illness and death (Mrs. Marlin) left Monday for Brownwood.

Marriage Record of Ardelia "Delia" May Davis and Christopher Columbus "Lum" Marlin

Ardelia May "Delia" Davis Marlin

**Ardelia May, Baby Grace Irene, Leonard
Stephen and Christopher Colombus
"Lum" Marlin**

Ardelia May Davis

Christopher Colombus "Lum" Marlin
Est. age 16 years old

Ardelia May Davis Marlin

William Davis Beck
Child of Nancy Ann Mourning Davis
Grandchild of William Thomas Davis
Great-Grandchild of William Henry Davis
March 29, 1825 – DOB
September 18, 1871 – DOD

William Davis Beck was the son of Nancy Ann Mourning Davis Beck. William was born in 1825 in Jones County, Georgia. William Davis served as a Confederate Captain in Company D, 2nd Mississippi Infantry.

On March 2, 1871, William married Ann Eliza Moorman. Ann was born in 1845 and died in 1921.

Per records, William Davis and Ann Eliza had the following children: Samuel M. and Willie Moorman Beck.

William Davis Beck died in 1871 in Benton County, Mississippi.

William Davis Beck

(CONFEDERATE.)

B.	2nd.	Miss

W. D. Beck

Capt. 2nd. Miss.

Appears on a
LIST
of officers killed and wounded, of
the 2d Corps, in the battle of
Manassas, Va., July 21, 1861.

List dated. Fairfax Co. Ho
Sept. 21, 1861 , 186

Commander Col. Faulkner.
Casualty Wounded July 21, 1861
Remarks

Casualties, Va., 265.

F.H.
Copyist.

William Davis Beck

B

2   Miss.

W. D. Beck

Capt. , Co. B , 2 Reg't Mississippi Infantry.

Appears on

Company Muster Roll

of the organization named above,

for *March & April* , 186 2

Enlisted :

When _____ , 186 __ .

Where _____

By whom _____

Period _____

Last paid :

By whom _____

To what time _____ 186 __ .

Present or absent _____

Remarks: *Discharged*

Book mark :

J. B. Ford

(642)

William Davis Beck

B | 2 | Miss.

William D. Beck

Capt. , Co. D , 2 Reg't Mississippi Infantry.

Appears on

Company Muster Roll

of the organization named above,

for _July & Aug_ , 186_1_ .

Enlisted:
When _April 27_ , 186_ .
Where _Pine Grove_
By whom _Col. W. C. Falkner_
Period _1 year_

Last paid:
By whom _Capt. Wm. Barksdale_
To what time _June 30_ , 186_ .

Present or absent _Present_

Remarks: _Wounded at Manassas July 21, in battle all day_

Book mark: _____

(842) _J. S. Dowd_ Copyist.

William Davis Beck

John Thomas Beck
Child of Nancy Ann Mourning Davis
Grandchild of William Thomas Davis
Great-Grandchild of William Henry Davis
April 3, 1827 – DOB
April 4, 1903 – DOD

John Thomas was the son of Nancy Ann Mourning Davis. John Thomas was born in 1827 in Bedford County, Tennessee. John Thomas was a Confederate soldier with the 18th Regiment Mississippi Calvary.

On February 19, 1856, John Thomas married Rebecca Ann Lewis in Tappah, Mississippi. Rebecca was born in 1839 and died in 1902.

Per records, John Thomas and Rebecca had the following children: Martha Elizabeth, Emily Elizabeth, John Benjamin, Darthula Rebecca, Viora Eugenia and James Orrin Emasy Beck.

John Thomas Beck died on April 4, 1903 in Pine Grove, Benton County, Mississippi.

John Thomas Beck

(CONFEDERATE.)

C 1 18 Miss

John T. Beck

Pvt. Co. A. 18 Rgt. Miss

Appears on a Report of the

**Medical Examining Board,
Dalton, Georgia,**

under the head of "Examination for fur-
loughs."

Brigade _McLaughlin_
Division
Army
Captain
When made _Feby. 21_ , 1865.
Number of days _60_
Hospital _Gunnison_
Last paid , 186 .
Disability _Granular Conjunctivitis
of one year standing_

Town _Selma_
County _Tippah_
State _Miss_
Remarks:

Confed. Arch., Chap. 6, File No. 543, page _76_.

R. B. Duncan

(605)   Copyist.

John Thomas Beck

Joshua Emasy Beck
Child of Nancy Ann Mourning Davis
Grandchild of William Thomas Davis
Great-Grandchild of William Henry Davis
February 1829 – DOB
September 10, 1901 – DOD

Joshua Emasy Davis was the son of Nancy Ann Mourning Davis. Joshua Emasy was born in 1829 in Bedford County, Tennessee.

Around the year 1855, Joshua Emasy married Lucy Ann Nooner in Tappah County, Mississippi. Lucy was born in 1834 and died in 1874.

Per records, Joshua and Lucy had the following children: Judge, Mary Ophelia, Nathan Emasy, Francis Owen, Samuel L., John Joshua "Johnny", Lucy A., and Robert L. Beck.

Joshua Emasy Davis was a Confederate Soldier. He enlisted on May 3, 1862 at Grand Junction, Tennessee for a period of three years. He was a Private in Company K 37th Regiment, Mississippi Infantry.

Around April 9, 1865, this regiment was consolidated with the 24th, 27th, 29th and 30th Regiments Mississippi Infantry, and formed a new regiment which was designated the 24th Regiment Mississippi Infantry.

Joshua Emasy Davis died on September 10, 1901 and is buried in the Beck Family Cemetery in Marshall, Mississippi.

Joshua Emasy Beck
Beck Family Cemetery -
Mississippi

75 | **34** | **Miss.**

Joshua E. Beck

Pire , Co. *K* , 37 Reg't Mississippi Inf.*

Appears on

Company Muster Roll

of the organization named above,

for *dated Oct. 31* , 186*2*

Enlisted :

When *May 3* , 186*2*

Where *Grand Junction, Tenn.*

By whom *Ben Lox*

Period *3 years or the war.*

Last paid:

By whom

To what time , 186

Present or absent *Present*

Remarks: *No bounty paid*

*This company subsequently became Company *K*, 34th Regiment Mississippi Infantry.

The 34th Regiment Mississippi Infantry was organized in April, 1862, as the 37th Regiment Mississippi Infantry. By S. O. No. 31, Headquarters Department No. 2, dated March 6, 1863, the designation was changed to the 34th Regiment Mississippi Infantry, that being the number by which this regiment was known at the Confederate War Department.

About April 9, 1865, this regiment was consolidated with the 24th, 27th, 29th and 30th Regiments Mississippi Infantry, and formed a new regiment which was designated the 24th Regiment Mississippi Infantry.

Book mark :

W. W. Wilkey

(645) Copyist.

Joshua Emasy Beck

Fredonia Ann Beck
Child of Nancy Ann Mourning Davis
Grandchild of William Thomas Davis
Great-Grandchild of William Henry Davis
November 9, 1836 – DOB
April 29, 1862 – DOD

Fredonia Ann Beck was the daughter of Nancy Ann Mourning Davis Beck. Fredonia was born in 1836 in Bedford County, Tennessee. On December 18, 1855, Fredonia married Thomas G. Toombs in Tippah, Mississippi. Thomas G. Toombs was born in 1825.

Per records, Fredonia and Thomas had the following children: Mary Elizabeth "Bettie", Charles W. "Charley", and Thomas Arthur Toombs.

Fredonia Ann Beck Toombs died in 1862. Fredonia was only 25 years old at the time of her death.

Fredonia Ann Beck Toombs

George Granberry Davis
Child of James Gresham Davis
Grandchild of James Sherwood Davis
Great-Grandchild of William Henry Davis
September 23, 1840 – DOB
January 13, 1917 – DOD

George Granberry Davis was the son of James Gresham Davis. George was born in 1840 in Fayette, Georgia. George was a soldier in the Civil War per 1861-1865 war records. He fought in the 27th Battalion, Georgia Infantry Company E during the Civil War.

On December 19, 1865, George married Mary Elizabeth Riser in Harris County, Georgia. Mary Elizabeth was born in 1845 and died in 1876.

Per records, George and Mary had the following children: Fannie Bell, George William, Marion Grissom and Adolphus Decatur Davis.

George Granberry Davis died in 1917 in Folkston, Chartton, Georgia. George is buried at Pineview Cemetery in Folkston, Georgia.

Excerpt from the book Charlton County Georgia: Historical Notes by John Harris

• One of the earliest members of the Davis family to come to America from England was Thomas Davis. He arrived on the "Margaret" in James City, Virginia, in 1619.He is believed to have been the grandson of Sir Thomas Davisof the London Company. He married Elizabeth Pierpont. Before the end of the 17th century branches of the Davis family were to be found in many communities surrounding the Chesapeake Bay as well as in Delaware and Pennsylvania. James Grissom Davis born 1806, married Ronnie Davis, who was also born in 1806. They settled in Harris Count , GA. They had four children, Roxie Ann, 1831; Adolphus, 1833; William Thornton, 1837; and George Granberry, born September 6, 1840. He Married Mary Elizabeth Riser, born 1845, on December 19, 1865 in Harris County. Their first child Fannie Belle, married Albert Wallace Askew.

Mary Elizabeth and George Granberry Davis

George Granberry Davis Pineview Cemetery in Folkston, Georgia

RE-CREATION OF ORIGINAL PHOTO
Family of George Granberry Davis

A Festive Day in the Askew-Davis Home in Harris County, Georgia

Front row: Adolphus "Dol" Davis (25), George Granberry "Pa" Davis (59), Albert Leon Askew (5), Fannie Belle Davis (32), Baby Andrew Newton "Newt" Askew (3mos.), Esther Kathleen Askew (3), Albert Wallace "Papa" Askew (35), George William "Uncle Bill" Davis (30)
Back row: Marion Grisson "Gris" Davis (27), Fred Davis Askew (8), Mary "Sister" Bessie Askew (13), Archibald Roy Askew (10)
March 1899

George Washington Davis
Child of William Columbus Davis
Grandchild of James Sherwood Davis
Great-Grandchild of William Henry Davis
January 31, 1838 – DOB
January 5, 1917 – DOD

George Washington Davis was the son of William Columbus Davis. George was born in 1838 in Randolph County, Alabama.

On August 7, 1860, George married Minnie Malinda Foreman in Rusk Texas. Minnie was born in 1840 and died in 1906.

Per records, George and Minnie had the following children: Joseph R., Frank, Marshall Abner, George L., George Elias, James A. and Thomas J. Davis.

George Washington Davis died in 1917 in Wichita Texas.

George Washington Davis and Minnie Malinda Foreman Davis

GEORGE W. DAVIS
MINNIE M. FOREMAN

George Washington Davis and Minnie Malinda Foreman Davis

Marshall Abner Davis and Family (child
of George Washington Davis)
Nettie Mae Davis, Marshall Abner
Davis, Richard Owen Davis, Bessie
Irene Davis, Bernetta Mae Williamson
Davis, Sarah E. Davis

Charles G. Lyle
Child of Sarah Jane Davis
Grandchild of James Sherwood Davis
Great-Grandchild of William Henry Davis
December 17, 1837 – DOB
March 12, 1929 – DOD

Charles G. Lyle was the son of Sarah Jane Davis Lyle. Charles was born in 1837 in Harris County, Georgia. In 1857, Charles married Frances E. Bracewell in Harris County, Georgia. Frances was born in 1835 and died in 1900.

Charles was a Confederate soldier with Company E, 46th Regiment Georgia Volunteer Infantry.

Per records, Charles and Frances had the following children: Sarah Almeda "Sallie", James Garfield and Ema Lyle.

Charles died in 1929 at the age of 91 years old. He died in a Confederate Soldiers' Home in Atlanta, Georgia. Charles is buried at Forrest Park in Georgia.

- Company E, 46th Regiment Georgia Volunteer Infantry
Harris County

"Harris Blues"
Lyle, Charles G. -- Private - March 4, 1862. On detached duty, teamster with supply train near Newberry, South Carolina, May 1, 1865. (Born in Harris County, Georgia December 17, 1837. Died in Confederate Soldiers' Home, at Atlanta, Georgia March 12, 1929. Buried at Forest Park, Georgia.)

This company left Griffin, Georgia for Pocataligo, South Carolina. From thence went to Coosawhatchie and the vicinity of Grahamville, South Carolina, April 30, 1862; thence to Charleston and to James Island and Secessionville, South Carolina, June 30, 1862. Ordered to Charleston and encamped at White Point Garden, October 22, 1862; to Pocataligo October 1862. Returned to Charleston October 27, 1862; to Wilmington, North Carolina, December 14, 1862; to Charleston December 29, 1862; again to Wilmington. Returned to Charleston February 11, 1863. Ordered to Jackson, Mississippi, and engaged the enemy near that city May 14, 1863. From there to Calhoun Station, 20 miles distant; to Canton,

Mississippi, 16 miles; to Yazoo City, Mississippi, 33 miles; thence near Vernon, Mississippi, 26 miles, June 1863. Engaged the enemy at Missionary Ridge, Tennessee, November 25, 1863. Removed to camp near Dalton, Georgia, leaving Kennesaw Mountain, Georgia July 2, 1864. Skirmished with enemy near Chattahoochee River until July 8, 1864. Fell back to Atlanta, Georgia, July 18, 1864. Met enemy at Peachtree Creek, Georgia July 21, 1864, and at Atlanta, Georgia July 22, 1864. Ordered to Poplar Springs Creek August 27, 1864; thence to East Point, thence to Jonesboro, Georgia August 30, 1864.

• Notes for CHARLES G. LYLE:
died at a private sanitarium Tuesday afternoon, March 12, 1929, in his ninety first year. He is survived by his daughters: Mrs. Delia Brown, Mrs. Sallie Darnell, Kenwood, GA; and son, Mr. B G Lyle; son in law, Mr. Eugenis Wooten, Jonesboro, Ga and brother Mr. James Davis "Jim" Lyle, Carrollton, GA. Lyle, Charles G. - Confederate, Private, March 4, 1862. On detached duty, teamster with supply train near Newberry, S.C., May 1, 1865. Born Harris Co., Ga. December 17, 1837. Died in Confederate Soldier's Home, at Atlanta, Ga.

March 12, 1929. Buried at Forrest Park, Ga. His father was Charles L. Lyle - Burial place unknown.

**Charles G. Lyle holding
Grandchild**

James Davis "Jim" Lyle
Child of Sarah Jane Davis
Grandchild of James Sherwood Davis
Great-Grandchild of William Henry Davis
March 22, 1844 – DOB
May 25, 1930 – DOD

James Davis "Jim" Lyle was the son of Sarah Jane Davis Lyle. James was born in 1844 in Cullman County, Alabama.

- American Civil War Soldiers

American Civil War Soldiers
Name: James D Lyle ,
Residence: Harris County, Georgia
Enlistment Date: 15 Aug 1861
Side Served: Confederacy
State Served: Georgia
Service Record: Enlisted as a Private on 15 August 1861
Enlisted in Company H, 17th Infantry Regiment Georgia on 15 August 1861.
Surrendered Company H, 17th Infantry Regiment Georgia on 09 April 1865 in Appomattox Court House, VA

-

- James D. "Bud" Lyle born March 22, 1844 in Georgia. He fought in the Civil War. He volunteered for the army before he was old enough to be conscripted. He did not have a Confederate uniform so several of the neighbors gathered. They sheared the sheep; worked and dyed the wool; carded, batted, spun the thread, wove the cloth and made his uniform in three days, and he left for the war. He was with General Robert E. Lee where He surrendered at Appomattox Court House. After the war he came back to Georgia and married and reared a large family. One of his girls was named Shellie. She married a Little. Source: Ida Lyle, Rt. 1, Tremont, Mississippi
- Jim lost two fingers at the battle of Gaines Mill , Hanover Co., Virginia in a skirmish, as researched by Roy Stallings lll , after a battle the company was at a stream when they "got into it" with some Yankees. It is reported that Jim was hit in the hand by a rifle(?) ball.

After the war, James went back to Georgia where he married and raised a large family. On January 14, 1868, James married Nancy Maryann Champion. Nancy was born in 1851 and died in 1935.

Per records, James and Nancy had the following children: William Philemon, James Monroe, John Thomas "Tom", Sandal Beulah, Shillie Josephine, Berryman Adam Hiram "Ira", Henry Bartlett, Frances Jane "Fannie", Grover Cleveland, Eugene Byron, Roy Judson, Samuel Calvin and Mosley Champion "Champ" Lyle.

• 1926 Confederate Memorial Day

In this 1926 photo of Confederate Soldiers, Jim Lyle is seated in the center front row. If you notice his right leg it's not real. Not due to wounds from the war but; Daddy said;" Sometime after Jim and Nancy's eleventh child was born, Jim was at work pulling logs out out of the woods on a cart pulled by horses, when a wheel of the cart ran over him. He lost his right leg as a result of the accident.
Willie Philemon, was their first born, then Monroe, who went to work on the

railroad when he was 21 and made it his career. Ira, was a preacher, changed denominations at least seven times. Tom was next, then Grover, they both farmed all of their lives. Byron was 18 years old when he was struck by lightening and Henry died of the fever when he was a small boy. Calvin was mentally retarded and never moved away from home. When he was 54 years old, he went out on the porch to chase off a barking dog in the dark. He tripped and fell off the porch, breaking his foot. He died the same night. Champ, short for Champion, was the youngest boy. He worked in the coal mine in Birmingham for a while. When he lived about six miles out in the country from Bremen, Ga. he would jump on a train and ride into town, when the train was leaving town he'd jump into an empty boxcar then as the train got close to his house he'd jump off in the bushes. Until one day, as he was going to hop a train his foot went down on the track. The train wheels cut his foot half off. Beaulah married George Spence. He died when she was pregnant with their second child. Shillie married Willis Little and Fannie married Will Walker. I've left out

Uncle Roy, Roy Judson, him and Byron
was about the same age, I
think."

- ## Oak Grove Church Pays Tribute
  ## to James D. Lyle

At the closing of the 25th day of May
1930, Brother James D. Lyle, took his
departure from this world of sin and sorrow to
a home for those who love God. Brother Lyle
was born March 22,1844. In 1867 he united
with the Missionary Baptist Church in Harris
County from which he moved his membership
to Oak Grove Baptist Church, where he
remained a member until his death. He was
married to Miss Nannie Mary Champion
January 14, 1868. To this union were born
thirteen children, two having proceeded him
to the grave several years ago.

The children who survive him are: W.
P. Lyle; G. C Lyle; R. J. Lyle; S. C. Lyle; M.
C. Lyle; Mrs. S. B. Spence of Carrollton
Route 3; J. T. Lyle of Villa Rica; J. M. Lyle
of Choffee, Mo.; B. A. Lyle, Carrollton,
Route 4; Mrs. W.L. Little, Clem Route 1; Mrs.
W. S. Walker, Roopville Route 2.

Brother Lyle served four years as a
volunteer for his country. Not only did he
serve his country but we that knew his daily
life know that he served his God. Brother
Lyle's life is a beautiful example of patience,

love, devotion and loyalty which, we should all strive to follow. Therefore we as a committee can say "Blessed are the dead which die in the Lord.

Dear brother thou hast left us
With sad and breaking hearts,
But in heaven we hope to meet you
Where we never
more shall part.

1. Resolved that the church has lost a noble member. 2. Resolved that a copy of this be put on the church record and a copy be submitted to the county papers for publication.

W. C. Cottle, W. B. Griffin, J. A. Grizzard, Committee, May 25th, 1930

(CONFEDERATE)

| I | 17 | Ga. |

James Lyle

Pvt., Co. H., 17 Reg't., Ga. Vols.

Appears on a

REPORT

of casualties, in the 17th Reg't.
Ga. Vols., in the battle of Garnett's
Farm, Va., June 27, 1862, and Malvern
Hill, Va., July 1, 1862.

Report dated Camp near Darbytown Road
July 24 186 2.

Date June 27 ,186 .
Remarks: wounded

Series 1, Vol. 11, part 2, page 703.

SEAronstein

( )
Copyist.

1371

James Davis Lyle

L   17   Ga.

J. D. Lyle

Corp , Co. H , 17 Reg't Georgia Infantry,

Appears on

Company Muster Roll

of the organization named above,

for *July & Aug* , 1864.

Enlisted:

When _____ *Aug 20* , 1861.

Where _____ *Harris Co*

By whom _____ *Capt Kennon*

Period _____ *war*

Last paid:

By whom _____ *Capt. Shorter*

To what time _____ *July 1* , 1864.

Present or absent _____ *Present*

Remarks:

Book mark:

(442) _____ *L a Boyd* _____ *Copyist*

L   17   Ga.

James Lyle

Pvt , Co. H , 17 Reg't Georgia Infantry,

Appears on

Company Muster Roll

of the organization named above,

for *Jany & Feby* , 1863.

Enlisted:

When _____ *Aug 20* , 186 .

Where _____ *Harris Cty*

By whom _____ *R. E. Kennon*

Period _____ *war*

Last paid:

By whom _____ *C. W. Math*

To what time _____ *Jany 1* , 186 .

Present or absent _____ *Present*

Remarks:

Book mark:

(442) _____ *L a Boyd* _____ *Copyist*

(OVER

James Davis Lyle

The Confederate States, Dr.

Dr. *James Lyle*

Private of Co. "K" 17th ___ Reg. ___ C. S. Army,

	DOLLAR.	CENT.
For Monthly Pay, from *January 1st* 1862 to *October 31* 1862 being .....*10*.... Months. .... Days, at ....*11*.... per month,	110	00
For Clothing.............................	25	00
For Use and Risk		
Dollars, Due.................		
Amount Paid	135	00

I certify that I have Endorsed this Payment on....*James Lyle*
Private of C. "K" .... of his Reg.....Descriptive Bill.

Maillard

____ Captain and A. Q. M.

RECEIVED, *Columbus* this *25* day of *November* 1862 from Major F. W. Dillard, Quartermaster C. S. Army, the sum of.........................
One Hundred & thirty five .... Dollars, being the Amount, and in full of the above Account.

James D. Lyle

Witness,

James Davis Lyle

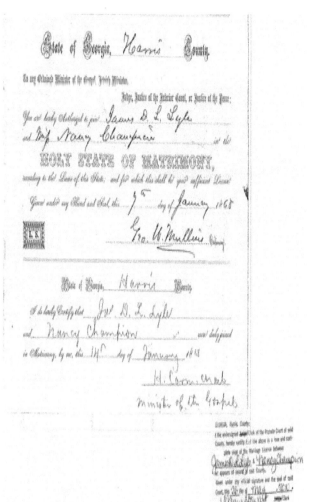

Marriage Certificate of James Davis Lyle and Nancy MaryAnn Champion

LOCAL

Confederate veterans in 1925

In recognition of Confederate Memorial Day which was yesterday, April 26, this picture was submitted for publication by Iris Jones. It was taken in 1925 in front of the Coca-Cola plant in Carrollton. All the men are Confederate veterans and all were 80 years or over. Front row, from left; Jim Kugler, Mr. Bloodworth, Johnny Brice, Mr. Pitts, George Cheney, Jim Lyle, John Mulliner. Back row, from left; George Harper, Mr. Huey, Clay Reeves, Billy Spence, Tom Jackson, W.O. Ferry, Mr. Moore, Mr. Aldridge, Mr. Bowen.

James Lyle and Confederate Veterans

**Confederate Veterans
James "Jim" Lyle is on the front
row, second from right end. He
holds two walking canes.**

James Davis Lyle and Nancy Champion Lyle with their children – 1915
Front Row: Left to Right Samuel Calvin Lyle, Roy Judson Lyle, & Mosely Champion "Champ" Lyle
Middle Row: Left to Right James Davis Lyle, Nancy Mary Ann Champion Lyle, William "Willie" Philemon Lyle, James Monroe Lyle, John Thomas "Tom" Lyle
Back Row: Left to Right Grover Cleveland Lyle, Frances "Fannie" Jane Lyle Walker, Berryman Adam Hiram "Ira" Lyle, Shillie Josephene Lyle Little, & Sandal Beaulah Lyle Spence
_ Sons already Deceased when this photo was made Henry Bartlett Lyle 1880-1881, & Eugene Byron Lyle 1887-1905

James and Nancy Lyle

James Davis Lyle and Nancy Lyle
Oak Grove Baptist Church

**Martha Melissa Davis
Child of Lewis Franklin Davis
Grandchild of Joshua Davis
Great-Grandchild of William
Henry Davis
October 5, 1841 – DOB
July 9, 1908 – DOD**

Martha Melissa Davis was the daughter of Lewis Franklin Davis. Martha was born in 1841 in Heard County, Georgia. On November 13, 1859, Martha married William Morrow Wood. William was born in 1830 and died in 1902.

Per records, Martha and William had the following children: Joseph B., Mary Elizabeth "Molly", Lela B., William Franklin, Lewis Young, Todd M. and John Andrew Wood.

Martha died in 1908 in Cherokee County, Georgia.

**Martha Melissa Davis
Rehoboth Community
Cemetery**

Mary Elizabeth Davis
Child of Lewis Franklin Davis
Grandchild of Joshua Davis
Great-Grandchild of William
Henry Davis
April 8, 1844 – DOB
September 30, 1907 – DOD
    Mary Elizabeth Davis was the daughter of Lewis Franklin Davis. Mary was born in 1844 in Georgia. On September 13, 1865, Mary married Erasmus Henry "Ras" Lipham. Erasmus was born in 1839 and died in 1920.

    Per records, Mary and Erasmus had the following children: Sarah Elizabeth, Lewis John, Martha Emily, William Martin, James Andrew, Amanda, Beulah L., Belle and Burton Irving Lipham.

    Mary Elizabeth died in 1907 in Cleburne, Alabama.

**Erasmus Henry and Mary Elizabeth
Davis Lipham
1880**

**Mary Elizabeth Davis Lipham
Mt. Peran Baptist Church
Cemetery in Cleburne, Alabama**

**Mt Peran Baptist Church
Cemetery in Cleburne, Alabama**

Martin Joshua Davis
Child of Lewis Franklin Davis
Grandchild of Joshua Davis
Great-Grandchild of William Henry Davis
July 5, 1845 – DOB
October 13, 1916 – DOD

Martin Joshua Davis was the son of Lewis Franklin Davis. Martin was born in 1845 in Heard County, Georgia. Martin was named after his grandfather, Joshua Davis.

On March 10, 1870, Martin married Amanda Evans "Mandy" Lane. Amanda was born in 1850 and died in 1931. Martin Joshua moved from Georgia to Texas and farmed the lands for many years.

Per records, Martin and Amanda had the following children: Sarah Elizabeth, Ida Lee, Lewis Joseph "Joe", and William Thomas "Will" Davis.

Martin Joshua died in 1916 in Gainesville, Cooke County, Texas.

Martin Joshua Davis
Fairview Cemetery in Gainesville,
Texas

Death Certificate of Martin Joshua Davis

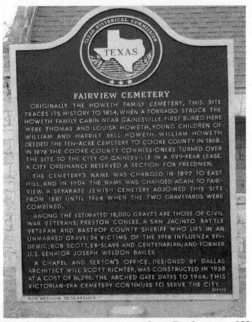

FAIRVIEW CEMETERY

ORIGINALLY THE HOWETH FAMILY CEMETERY, THIS SITE TRACES ITS HISTORY TO 1854, WHEN A TORNADO STRUCK THE HOWETH FAMILY CABIN NEAR GAINESVILLE. FIRST BURIED HERE WERE THOMAS AND LOUISA HOWETH, YOUNG CHILDREN OF WILLIAM AND HARRIET BELL HOWETH. WILLIAM HOWETH DEEDED THE TEN-ACRE CEMETERY TO COOKE COUNTY IN 1868. IN 1878 THE COOKE COUNTY COMMISSIONERS TURNED OVER THE SITE TO THE CITY OF GAINESVILLE IN A 999-YEAR LEASE. A CITY ORDINANCE RESERVED A SECTION FOR FREEDMEN.

THE CEMETERY'S NAME WAS CHANGED IN 1897 TO EAST HILL, AND IN 1904 THE NAME WAS CHANGED AGAIN TO FAIRVIEW. A SEPARATE JEWISH CEMETERY ADJOINED THIS SITE FROM 1881 UNTIL 1964 WHEN THE TWO GRAVEYARDS WERE COMBINED.

AMONG THE ESTIMATED 18,000 GRAVES ARE THOSE OF CIVIL WAR VETERANS; PRESTON CONLEE, A SAN JACINTO BATTLE VETERAN AND BASTROP COUNTY SHERIFF WHO LIES IN AN UNMARKED GRAVE; 34 VICTIMS OF THE 1918 INFLUENZA EPIDEMIC; BOB SCOTT, EX-SLAVE AND CENTENARIAN; AND FORMER U.S. SENATOR JOSEPH WELDON BAILEY.

A CHAPEL AND SEXTON'S OFFICE, DESIGNED BY DALLAS ARCHITECT WILL SCOTT RICHTER, WAS CONSTRUCTED IN 1938 AT A COST OF $6,296. THE ARCHED GATE DATES TO 1964. THIS VICTORIAN-ERA CEMETERY CONTINUES TO SERVE THE CITY. (1999)

RON MELUGIN, RESEARCHER

Fairview Cemetery in Gainesville, Texas
Burial place of Martin Joshua Davis

William Owen Davis
Child of Lewis Franklin Davis
Grandchild of Joshua Davis
Great-Grandchild of William Henry Davis
February 26, 1847 – DOB
December 5, 1941- -DOD

William Owen Davis was the son of Lewis Franklin Davis. William was born in 1847 in Heard County, Georgia. William was a soldier in the Confederate Army during the latter part of the Civil War. He served as a Private in Company K, 56th Regiment of Georgia Volunteers.

After the Civil War, the urge to go west was felt strongly in the Davis family. In 1870, William Owen traveled by boat, train, stage and foot to reach Gainesville, Texas where he practiced law and became a judge.

On September 25, 1873, William Owen married Harriet Isabella "Bella" Faver. Harriet was born in 1850 and died in 1885. On February 1, 1887, William Owen married Anna Lee Underwood. Anna Lee was born in 1864 and died in 1951.

Per records, William Owen had the following children: Isabella F., William Owen and Sarah E. Davis.

William Owen died in 1941 in Gainesville, Cooke County, Texas.

Georgia native W.O. Davis served in the Confederate Army and was admitted to the Georgia bar in 1870. He moved to Texas, settling in Gainesville, and was soon involved in local politics and civic life. In a long public service career, Davis served on the school board as a city Alderman and was a State Senator from 1882 to 1885. He later was Mayor of Gainesville at age 81. A prominent Cooke County attorney, Davis argued two cases before the U.S. Supreme Court.

William Owen Davis

**William Owen Davis
Fairview Cemetery in
Gainesville, Texas**

ANNA UNDERWOOD DAVIS
FEB 13. 1864
JULY 20. 1951

"SHE WALKED IN BEAUTY"

Second wife of William Owen Davis

Lewis Franklin "Dock" Jr. Davis
Child of Lewis Franklin Davis
Grandchild of Joshua Davis
Great-Grandchild of William Henry Davis
May 2, 1849 – DOB
November 15, 1938 – DOD

Lewis Franklin Jr. Davis was the son of Lewis Franklin Davis. Lewis was born in 1849 in Heard County, Georgia. On October 6, 1877, Lewis married Ettie Sophronia Cook. Ettie was born in 1855 and died in 1937.

Per records, Lewis and Ettie had the following children: Lena Emily, Lewis Franklin III, Hope Hull and Owen Cook Davis.

Lewis Franklin Jr. died in 1938 in Heard County, Georgia.

- The Roop Freshet by Jere R. Ridley
  - April 23, 1883 , Heard Co, GA
  - Copied from **History of** Heard **County 1830-1990 , published by The Heard County Historical Society**
  -
  -

The Roop Freshet

Merrell's Mill was a small, rural community in western Heard County on the Hillabahatchee Creek. It had its beginning in antebellum days, and by 1883 it had existed for decades as a self-sufficient hamlet. **Robert Merrell, Sr.** had established a thriving family business consisting of a large plantation, corn and wheat mills, gin, blacksmith's shop and store. **Mr. Merrell's daughter, Georgia**, married **Josephus (Ceph) Roop**, son of the founder of Roopville, Georgia. Mr. Ceph Roop, along with his brother, Mr. **T. M. (Bud) Roop**, were employed by Mr. Merrell to help manage the Merrell family enterprises at Merrell's Mill.

This mill site, along with the people who worked and lived here, was to fall prey to one of the most dreadful natural disasters ever to occur in Heard County. For several generations, this disaster was to be a principal topic of discussion wherever people gathered in Heard County.

Today, those who know the story of the Merrell's Mill tragedy are few in number. Still, the story has the power and capacity to hold both storyteller and listener spellbound as the plot builds. Mr. T.M. Roop lived in Roopville, approximately 10 miles distant, with his wife and two young children. He spent the weekdays with his brother and his wife, Mr. and Mrs. Ceph Roop, so that he could be near his work at the mill. On weekends, he returned to Roopville to be with his young family, returning early each Monday morning to his work. This time, April 22, 1883, for an unknown reason, he returned early Sunday evening – a mistake he was never able to rectify. Ceph and Georgia Roop had three small children: Beulah, age 6, Homer, age 2 1/2 , and Ella, 15 months.

Sunday, April 22, 1883, dawned clear and spring-like. The setting at the mill, except for the neat, well-kept buildings, was on of natural, pristine beauty. The shallow creek situated among rolling hills is bedded with millions of smooth, native stones. The water is generally clear, except for brief periods following rain, and is surprisingly cool even in the hot summer months. This is accounted for in part by the shade provided the stream bed by the giant water oaks, sycamores, blackgums, maple, bay, river birch, mountain laurel, and rhododendron which abound in the rich bottom lands of the Hillabahatchee.

On this typical spring Sunday morning, the Roops could have slept a bit longer than they would have during the week. Under old-fashioned conditions, a miller's work, if not constantly physically demanding, requires constant vigilance. At peak times, the grinding of corn or wheat may start before dawn and only stop for a few hours' sleep way into the night – only to resume again early the next morning. Then there were the store and gin, small patches of corn, beans, potatoes and other vegetables for which Mrs. Roop was probably responsible. The creek bottom land also provided 8 to 10 acres of pasture land lush in late April with native grasses. The family most likely kept a horse and perhaps a couple of cows with their calves here. These animals, along with the chickens and hogs, required a lot of attention.

This Sunday morning, following a hard-earned extra bit of sleep, made even better by the cool, fragrant spring air and sounds of the waterfall from the creek, the Roops probably enjoyed a country breakfast. This, in all likelihood, consisted of freshly ground flour for biscuits, salt-cured ham and bacon from Mr. Roop's smokehouse and freshly brewed coffee. Brown yard eggs scrambled in the drippings from the ham would have provided the final course for this Sunday ritual.

Nearby, New Hope Church could have been the sanctuary the young family visited for worship services this final Sunday together. The old-time hymns, the lively-delivered sermon, an opportunity to be with friends and neighbors, and chance for the family to be close together for an hour or so as the sermon were long was probably a highlight of the week.

Mr. Roop, more than likely, drove the family home from church in their buggy. At home, Mrs. Roop would have fired-up the wood stove with dry, split firewood for a Sunday dinner of fried chicken or perhaps fresh fried fish from the mill pond. Side orders could have consisted of green beans, turnip greens, corn muffins, dried apple pies, or perhaps hash, made from dried and smoked beef. Historically, the weather has been alternately cool and warm in Heard County in late April. Spring rains prevail at this time. Even today, creek waters on a sunny day can comfortably and joyfully be waded in at this time of year. One can imagine that the children spent a great deal of that Sunday afternoon in the white sand and shallow water just short of the mill pond. The older Roops probably napped and read or made a routine check of the matters in their business as the afternoon passed.

Pricilla Ridley was a 12-year-old black girl, employed by Mr. Roop as nurse to help with the children and housework. Her father, Mr. Harmon Ridley, knew work as well as anyone in Heard County. After all, he had brought himself out of slavery even before slavery ended, by hard work and knowing how to obtain this valuable commodity from others. In slave times, he was a hired supervisor of slaves. He was paid well, and during that time he was a successful landowner and farmer. His daughter, Pricilla, would learn to love the joys of living self-sufficiently, on her own power, by the sweat of the brow.

Pricilla cried on this Sunday afternoon as her father drove her back to Merrell's Mill. Some say she was homesick. Others say she had a premonition. A close friend, name unknown, of Mrs. Roop frequently spent several days at a time at the Mill. She had planned to begin another visit the afternoon of this Sunday, April 22, but was so overcome by a reported feeling closely similar to homesickness that she did not venture away from her parents' home near Simpson as scheduled.

Late afternoon came and, at the supper table, Mrs. Roop remarked as to how dark it was getting outside. Mr. T. M. Roop had just arrived from his home in Roopville, and he was very glad to have made shelter before the impending storm.

Great clouds were gathering as the family enjoyed social time together, oblivious to the fate that awaited them. Rain and hail soon began to fall. Lightning was so bright and long-lasting that it was possible to read the headlines of a newspaper even though when the lightning had subsided pitch black darkness was everywhere, within and without.

After a while, everyone retired to bed. "The rain fell furiously, the water came rushing down from every hilltop, accumulating in every ravine, thence to the branches and creeks, until branches became creeks and creeks became rivers."

About 3:25 a.m., Pricilla Ridley waked Mr. Ceph Roop with loud knocking at his upstairs bedroom door. "There's water on my floor, Mr. Roop, there's water on my floor." After hearing this several times, Mr. Roop dismissed her to her room thinking this was somehow connected to her apparent homesickness, observed earlier. In a few minutes, Pricilla was back at Mr. Roop's door fervently knocking and screaming that there was water all about her bed. Mr. Roop calmed and consoled Pricilla as best he could and sent her back to her room.

At about 3:30 a.m., Mr. T. M. Roop called to his brother and told him that there was water on the floor of his sleeping room. Mr. T. M. Roop supposed the roof was leaking and told his brother so. At the next moment, Pricilla was again banging on Mr. Ceph Roop's door pleading for some understanding of the situation. She screamed, "Mr. Roop, my bed is floating!"

In the meantime, the water level was rising very rapidly all over the first floor of the house. Mr. T. M. Roop asked his brother what he should do and he said, "Save yourself if you can." Pandemonium followed, but it was all over in ten minutes. Mrs. Roop, in great horror, was calling for help to her father, Mr. Robert Merrell. His house was located on high ground near the mill. He tried to reach her but could not as his canoe and bridge across the road had been washed away. He watched helplessly as the store house crumbled. Mr. Ceph Roop begged his wife to leave their abode immediately but she refused, expressing her determination to remain and be with their children.

"The house washed from its pillars down-stream and drifted above water for some 500 yards until it hit a cliff and busted asunder."

Mr. Roop, who had been securing himself in the second floor window of the house, was thrown into the torrent as the house washed from its foundation. He swam after the house and buried under the timbers when it crashed into the bluff. The screams of the victims could be heard distinctly back at the mill by those safely ashore. Mr. Roop surfaced miraculously and drifted amidst the broken timbers and logs and swift downstream current. He was finally able to catch hold of a limb of a tree and pull himself into the fork of the upper limbs, three-fourths of a mile away from the ill. He was cold, alone, shocked emotionally and physically, and worried about his family. Yet, after a rest, he swam 80 yards to land. Mr. T. M. Roop was either drowned or killed by falling timbers.

The next day, great search parties gathered to look for survivors and victims. Among the searchers were nearly neighbors and family members. **Mr. L. F. (Dock) Davis** was among those who searched for survivors in vain. Fortunately, all of the bodies of the drowned were found and laid to rest.

The Merrells thought they had built their house above the danger of high water. But the cloudburst that caused the creek to rise 25 feet above the low level mark could not be predicted. Another possible explanation for the flood expressed shortly after the occurrence was that the water spout occurring ¾ mile upstream.

Following the recovering period, Mr. Ceph Roop went to Texas where he remarried and raised a second family.

Merrell's Mill was rebuilt and was later called Roller's Mill. Mr. and Mrs. Olin Avery of Franklin ran this mill, in the employment of Mr. Warner Awbrey, under similar circumstances as the Roops and Merrells, from 1925 to 1942. Mr. Avery vividly recalled to this writer the race, the water-driven stones, the wilderness, the toll, and the good life in this rural, isolated and indescribably beautiful setting and unique period of time.

Today, all signs of the mill and home sites are gone. The sycamores remain along with other native trees and wild flowers. Hawks, deer and foxes appreciate the seclusion offered by the remote region.

A steep climb of 500 yards or so from the mill site up a westward hill will bring the interested observer to the one remaining artifact of this great tragedy: the cemetery containing the graves of Mrs. Roop and her three children, marked by a stone cutter's hand in local granite. By Jere R. Ridley

A **freshet** is a great rise or overflowing of a stream caused by heavy rains or melted snow

Andrew Smith Davis
Child of Lewis Franklin Davis
Grandchild of Joshua Davis
Great-Grandchild of William Henry Davis
April 29, 1856 – DOB
October 24, 1902 – DOD

Andrew Smith Davis was the son of Lewis Franklin Davis. Andrew was born in 1856 in Franklin, Heard County, Georgia. On January 7, 1890, Andrew married Mary Clementine "Clemmie" Jackson. Mary Clementine was born in 1858 and died in 1938.

Per records, Andrew and Mary Clementine had the following children: William Lewis "Will", Della Pearl, Thomas Bradley and Alonzo Smith "Dock" Davis.

Andrew Smith Davis died in 1902 in Glenn, Heard County, Georgia.

Grandfather's Pistol by Robert Lewis (Rel) Davis

It was a rather lonely graduation for me when I got my bachelor's degree from Wayland College out in the Texas Panhandle in Plainview. My parents were a thousand miles away, up in northeast Montana where my father had just been called to be pastor of a small church that would soon become all Native American and launch his career as an Indian Missionary. They couldn't afford the trip back to my graduation.

Most of my relatives were at least 350 miles away, and most of them simply didn't care. A college education was a rather superfluous attainment at best - something other people in other families got, and then only in order to become a physician or lawyer or something important - and certainly not for something as useless as a degree in liberal arts.

So it was a lonely time when I walked up to get my diploma from Dr. A. Hope Owen, college president. (I used to joke that when Dr. Owen handed out each diploma he would tell the graduate, "God bless you," but when he came to me, he said "Thank God!" It didn't really happen, of course. He said "God bless you" to me just like to everyone else - but it could very well have happened, considering the events of my senior year! But that's another story.)

One member of my family did show up at my graduation, however. Cousin Joe. He showed up in his faded sports-coat and tie and even brought a graduation gift, a shirt (which, incidentally, I kept and treasured for many years.) Cousin Joe - **Lewis Joseph Davis -**

was my grandfather's first cousin, which made him my first cousin twice removed, there being two generations between my grandfather's and mine. At that time he was living on his farm down in the small community of Cotton Center, which was just west of the tiny town of Hale Center - a few miles south of Plainview. He was no longer farming, however, being 80 years old. He provided the land, seeds and fertilizer and a local farmer sharecropped for him.

While I was at Wayland I would drive down to visit him from time to time, partly because he was family and I felt a duty to do so, but mainly because of the stories he told me about my grandfather, , who had died the year before I graduated. Cousin Joe told some great stories about my grandfather, **William Lewis Davis**, whom he knew as "Cousin Will" and who had been four years his junior.

He told about the time, in the first few years of the nineteenth century, when **Will** showed up at Joe's farm outside of Gainesville (the town in North Texas where I was born and where my grandfather would die). According to Cousin Joe, **Will** had been in a shoot-out (Joe called it a duel) with another man and the other man was killed. The man's father and two brothers had sworn a vendetta (that's the word Joe used) against my grandfather and he had been forced to leave Georgia and move west.

He went to Gainesville because he had family there, a couple of uncles and a number of cousins, including Cousin Joe. Joe gave him a job on his farm and helped him get back on his feet (and hide from avenging relatives of the man he killed.) As evidence, Joe showed me the pistol my grandfather had used to kill the man. It was a .32 caliber Colt automatic pistol. **Will** had given it to Joe in gratitude for taking him in.

Cousin Joe told other stories about my grandfather as well. According to him, my grandfather was the only person he'd ever known who could chase down a jackrabbit on foot and catch it barehanded! He said **Will** would begin chasing a rabbit and, knowing it always would run in a counter-clockwise circle, would run just to the left of the rabbit, making a shorter arc to the same place the rabbit was going. Such a feat required amazing stamina, of course, as well as many, many circles before spiraling in on the hapless rodent. It seemed to me then (as it does today) somewhat unbelievable.

As it turned out, it was no more unbelievable than the story about the duel and vendetta! Many years later, I visited my grandfather's home town, a little hamlet called Glenn in far west Georgia. There I met with a number of relatives. I haunted the Heard County courthouse over in Franklin. I went through old newspaper clippings at the library. Nothing about a duel. Nothing about my grandfather having killed a man. There was a germ of truth to the story, however. In fact, several germs of truth.

First, he did leave Georgia under a bit of a cloud. It all started with his father, and a "pigeon drop" scam. Will's father, **Andrew Smith Davis**, my great-grandfather, was apparently a very proud man. In 1902, he was a prosperous farmer, owning seven different farms both in Georgia and across the border in Alabama.

One day he went to "the big city" (which is this case was Atlanta) to buy supplies for the farm. While there he met up with a team of "confidence" operators working one of the oldest scams in the book. The "pigeon drop" scam involves a pretended finding of a fortune in cash, jewelry or the like, and the offer to share the find with the victim (in this case my great-grandfather) if only the victim will put up an amount of cash as "good faith" money. When the victim turns over his good-faith money, he is given the "fortune" wrapped in a package, with the assurance that the con artist will return soon and divide up the wealth. After much waiting, the victim realizes that no one is coming back, opens up the package, and discovers it to be filled with blank paper.

Now, we don't know exactly what kind of scam my great-grandfather ran into in Atlanta -- that is, what kind of "fortune" he thought he would be sharing - and we don't even know how much money he lost. All that is certain is that it wasn't enough money to ruin him. When he died, which was very soon and by his own hand, he still owned all his farms and considerable wealth.

No, it wasn't the loss of his fortune that bothered him. It was the loss of his pride. He gave his wife, my great-grandmother (**Mary Clementine Jackson Davis**), instructions on how to take care of his farm, walked out to the barn and calmly blew his brains out with a pistol.

The local paper, The Franklin News and Banner, ran the following item on Friday, October 31, 1902:

Committed Suicide: After Telling His Wife How To Manage His Business, Mr. Smith Davis Kills Himself

Last Friday morning, Mr. **Smith Davis** of Glenn, killed himself with a revolver. It is rumored that Mr. Davis had made some bad trades in which he lost big money. On Friday morning, he told his wife that he was going off and advised her how to manage his business. In a few moments, his wife missed him; and in another moment she heard the report of a pistol. When he was found he was not quite dead, but died in a few minutes. He had gone into an old barn and shot himself through the head, the ball entering the right temple and coming out through the left temple."

When this happened, my grandfather was then 20 years old, the oldest son. The death of his father apparently hit him quite hard, for from that time he began to drink heavily. About two years later he was charged with a series of misdemeanors by a county grand jury. The charges included:

... that the said **Will Davis** on the 16th day of September in the year 1904, in the County aforesaid, then and there unlawfully and in the presence of 'Mrs. W.A. Forbus and Mrs. Rosi Johnson, did use without provocation the following profane language: "God-damn it I have been run over up yonder by **John Crouch**. "

... did then and there unlawfully have and carry about his person concealed and not in an open manner and fully exposed to view a certain pistol.

... did by being intoxicated, vomiting, cursing and using profane and obscene language and by loud and boisterous talking interrupt and disturb an assemblage and meeting of Glenn Public School for the purpose of scientific, literary and social improvement.

(I have copies of all the court procedures. The **"John Crouch**" mentioned in the indictment was another first cousin of his.) **Will** pled guilty to the charges and was sentenced to pay a fine of $35 (a lot of money in those days) or to be sent to a chain gang. He paid the fine by selling his farms - the inheritance from his father. Also sold (to his brother-in-law **I.Q. Adams** and his mother, **Clemmie Davis**) were 50 acres in cotton and 25 acres in corn, two mules ("a black horse mule named Bill" and "a mouse colored horse mule named Tobe"), a "Top buggy, Studebaker make, size two & three quarters," and even his cooking stove.

He left Georgia in 1905 and returned (as far as we can tell) only once more. Where he went, no one is sure. He later told about working on a fishing boat in Galveston, and about traveling around Texas using an assumed name. There is one story that he "married" an Indian woman and had several children by her.

He eventually ended up in Gainesville, Texas, working for Cousin Joe, and giving Joe his .32 caliber automatic. Was this the same pistol he waved in front of the night class in Glenn, Georgia? Was it the same one his father had used to take his own life? I don't know.

But I could find no story about a "duel" or a "vendetta," though those certainly make a much more interesting story than getting drunk and throwing up in front of a night school class! And I never could find any proof about his rabbit-chasing abilities either.

There was a shoot-out, however, but it wasn't between my grandfather and another man. It involved his brother (my great-uncle) and it took place more than a decade later. Was Cousin Joe confusing the two stories? The later story did involve my grandfather -- in one way or another. What happened was this:

After the death of her husband, my great-grandmother "Clemmie" moved to Texas with her two youngest sons, **Brad (Thomas Bradley)** and **"Dock" (Alonzo Smith**), who were both teenagers. She stayed in a house owned by one of her brothers-in-law. When the two boys became adults and were married, however, they decided to return to Georgia to manage the land still owned by the family. **Brad** set up a general store in Glenn community and Dock apparently managed the several farms.

Dock was notorious as a ladies' man and bad blood developed between himself and another man named **Dink Swint**, who was apparently a mulatto. Some stories say that Dink owed Dock some money. Some say he owed labor. Some say Swint was upset because Dock had been having an affair with his wife or girlfriend. Whatever the reason (and in my family the prevalent story is that Dock had loaned money to Swint over the winter in anticipation of his work in the spring, but in the spring Swint preferred to work for "real" money for other farmers), Dock and a cousin (**Willie Smith Adams**, son of the **I.Q. Adams** who bought my grandfather's farm) drove out to Swint's place for a show-down.

This was on January 30, 1919, and the very fact that Dock owned a large automobile is an indication that he was fairly well-to-do. Dock was armed, by the way. Dock parked his car a short way from the house where - it turned out - Dirk was holed up with a relative, both armed as well. As **Dock** and **Willie Smith** walked up to the house, gunfire erupted from two sources, the front door and an upstairs window. Dock was mortally wounded immediately and he gave his gun to Willie Smith, who returned the fire. The Swint relative behind the front door was killed in the gunfire. **Dirk Swint**, who had been firing from a second-floor window, fled out back.

Willie Smith, though badly injured with an arm wound, carried Dock to the car and drove back to town. **Dock** was dead by the time they got to Glenn. Willie Smith suffered from an infection due to the wound and when he died a few years later, it was apparently from the old gunshot wound.

Here's where my grandfather came into the picture. He was living back in Texas at this time, was married to my grandmother and settled in on a farm, and they already had five children. But he was the older brother and felt he had to go back to Georgia and "settle the score." He went to Georgia, armed, and stayed with another cousin (apparently a **Birdsong** but I haven't been able to find out exactly who) and "rode up and down the roads like a madman" according to Glenn community tradition. According to tradition, he never found **Dirk Swint**, who had disappeared completely (1 can find no record of Dirk Swint after the gunfight took place.)

Now here's where the story gets murky. One of my cousins claims she heard her father (my dad's brother) talking about our grandfather catching Swint in Georgia, killing him, and dragging his body out into the marshes behind his horse. These days, my uncle denies ever telling that story, and

everyone in the family insists that grand-dad
never found his brother's killer. . .

**Andrew Smith Davis
Mt. Zion Cemetery**

Peter Taylor
Child of Mary Amanda Davis
Grandchild of Joshua Davis
Great-Grandchild of William Henry Davis
October 15, 1848 – DOB
February 13, 1922 – DOD

Peter Taylor was the son of Mary Amanda Davis Taylor. Peter was born in 1848 in Randolph County, Alabama. In 1874, Peter married Sarah Jane Mize. Sarah was born in 1849 and died in 1925.

Per records, Peter and Sarah had the following children: Infant Taylor, Robert Paschal, John William, David, Georgia Ann, Joseph Merrill "Joe", Homer Heflin and Franklin Benjamin Taylor.

Peter Taylor died in 1922 in Port Arthur, Jefferson County, Texas.

Peter Taylor

Peter Taylor

**Peter Taylor
Port Arthur, Texas**

Death Certificate of Peter Taylor

James Franklin Pittman
Child of Rebecca Balsora Davis
Grandchild of Joshua Davis
Great-Grandchild of William Henry Davis
September 14, 1847 – DOB
September 10, 1922 – DOD

James Franklin Pittman was the son of Rebecca Balsora Davis and William Alphonso Pittman. James was born in 1847 in Springfield, Alabama. James was a Confederate Soldier in 1865.

On February 16, 1871, James married Emily Mandeville Lee in Randolph County, Alabama. Emily was born in 1852 and died in 1929.

Per records, James Franklin and Emily had the following children: Mary Rebecca, Mary B., William B., Ollia, Olive, Arthur Franklin "Tuck", Arra Lena, Cumile, Edgar, Florence Odessa, Infant Pittman, Lillie Mae, Mattie Belle, George D., Maggie Smith, Kittie Violet, Katie Bernice and Violet Pittman.

James Franklin Pittman died in 1922 in Springfield, Alabama.

1861-1865 – Confederate Battle Flag

- Letter from Wm Alphonso Pittman to his son J F Pittman, Confederate Soldier in 1865 - For this letter I want to thank *The Davis Lee Family Home Page, created by Davis Emerson Lee*

-

A father writes his soldier son in this, the third letter lent The Press by Mrs. Pearse Seegar. The writer, W. A. Pittman, is the recipient of the first letter, written from Texas in 1858 and published in this paper three weeks ago. It is thought that the Jef Davis mentioned here is the younger son, the father of Misses Eris and Lucy Pittman and Mrs. Owen Ford, now living in the Springfield community.

At Home, January the 13, 1865
Dear Dear Son,

I received yours of the 5 of January, which gave me great satisfaction to learn that you was well. These few lines leavs myself with the rest of the family well at this time, hopeing these few lines may find you enjoying the same blessing. I was glad to hear that you was at Talladega. I was fearful that you had bin sent Mobeal.

Thare has nothing of importance turned up heare sence I rote before. brother J. M. **{Jeptha Mitchell Pittman}** was brought home and at the time I rote wee expected to bring him. Thare was none of the Stitts went to sea him buried but William. An **{Ann Stitt Pittman, Jeptha's wife}** never went. He was buried at our old place.

I have sold Mary and her child to Ben Faulkner for his land. I gave him two thousan dollars to boot for five hundred and sixty acors of land on the Tallapoocy river. Wee have not drawd ritings yet but I thinke he will not backe out. I thinke I have made a very fare trade. I thinke the land is worth eight thousan dollars.

If you get the chance to come home you had better come by Julafinna if the bridge is not washed away. Wee have had the biggest freek heare I ever saw in this countrey. The crceke was the foolest I ever saw it. It washt away a heep of fence and land two. Nearley all of the mills that I have heard from is broke.

I thinke it is a bad chance to get any of the boys to come to your company. I thinke that tha will not go to the war till tha are made. I thinke the boys that is seventeen will have to go to the serve before long, but tha have all got under seventeen.

T. S. has rented the Pollard place and movd his family out thare. I thinke P. O. will move to Heard on Hilabehather. I will try and ingage your leather. Martin says make good soldier. He. expects to join you after he gos to school this year.

Jef Davis **{Jefferson Davis Pittman, James' 4-yr-old brother}** says if you will come home (he) will give you the biges yam in the hill.

I must come to a close. Rite evry opportunity and I will do the same. We have done nothing yet towards starting to make a crop. The weather is so bad that wee can not worke. The collards is all kild. Wheat is vary small. I have kild all the hogs but the six little ones. Tha all was much better than I expected. One of the Eely hogs wade 215 lbs.

W. A. Pitman

Nancy Smith "Nan" Pittman
Child of Rebecca Balsora Davis
Grandchild of Joshua Davis
Great-Grandchild of William Henry Davis
April 6, 1855 – DOB
January 27, 1944 – DOD

Nancy Smith Pittman was the daughter of Rebecca Balsora Davis Pittman. Nancy was born in 1855 in Alabama.

In August of 1874, Nancy married William Thomas Lee Sr. William was born in 1854 and died in 1944.

Per records, Nancy and William had the following children: Nash, Bailey Alphonso, William Thomas Jr., Robert Edward "Bob", Milton T., Clay Pittman and Leon P. Lee.

Nancy died in 1944 near Rock Mills in Randolph County, Alabama.

Nancy Smith Pittman and husband William Thomas Lee

Picture in Scrapbook (cir 1929), taken at the home of William Thomas Lee in Roanoke, AL. Sitting from viewer'a right - George Washington Lee, child, Lucy Avery Lee, William Thomas Lee, Nancy Smith Pittman. First row standing, from viewer's right - unkown female, unknown male, child - William Claude Lee, Jr, William Claude Lee, Bessie Emerson Lee, Mary Alice Lee, Clay Pittman Lee. Second row standing, from viewer's right - Milton Franklin Lee, Hassie Pike Lee, unknown male, unknown female, Robert E. Lee, Carrie Hodge Lee.

Etta Jane Pittman
Child of Rebecca Balsora Davis
Grandchild of Joshua Davis
Great-Grandchild of William Henry Davis
February 14, 1864 – DOB
June 16, 1946 – DOD

Etta Jane Pittman was the daughter of Rebecca Balsora Davis Pittman. Etta Jane was born in 1864 in Randolph County, Alabama.

In 1879, Etta Jane married Andrew Jackson Weathers. Andrew was born in 1854 and died in 1925. Per records, Etta Jane and Andrew had the following children: Infant child, Eunice, William T., Addie Maude, Bertha Lee, Hattie Eunice, Henry Davis, Katie Bernice, Benjamin Franklin, Mary Jean, Ruth, Andrew Jackson, Etta Mae, Louise and Lucile Weathers.

Etta Jane Pittman Weathers died in 1946 in Wedowee, Randolph County, Alabama.

**Etta Jane Pittman
Weathers holding Benjamin**

1896 Andrew Jackson
Weathers   Family

c. 1896

Family members thought to be:
L-R: Henry,   William,
Andrew holding Katie; Bertha
Lee; Addie; Etta Jane holding
Benjamin; Hettie. They would
have six more children, 2 of
which died as infants.

William Franklin Lipham
Child of Sarah Sophronia Davis
Grandchild of Joshua Davis
Great-Grandchild of William Henry Davis
September 12, 1855 – DOB
October 25, 1889 – DOD

William Franklin Lipham was born in 1855 and was the eldest of nine children of John Monroe Lipham and Sarah Sophronia Davis. William Franklin was also known to his family and friends as "Buddy" and "Billy".

On October 22, 1874, William Franklin married Sarah Vida Lee. Some records have her listed as Sarah Victoria Lee. She was the fourth child out of thirteen children born to Isham Bailey Lee and Mary Alice Weathers. Sarah was born in 1856 and died in 1875. Sarah died from what was known as childbirth fever.

Sarah Vida Lee Lipham is buried, along with her parents, in the New Lee Family Cemetery at the home of her brother, Rev. Jesse Frank Lee, near Rock Mills, Randolph County, Alabama.

On September 23, 1877, William Franklin married Charlotte Stewart Merrill Reaves. William and Charlotte had ten children, only five of which lived past infancy. Charlotte was born in 1852 and died in 1928.

Per records, William Franklin Lipham had the following children: Hettie Beatrice, Georgia Ann, Charles Merrill, Maude M., Lloyd Cleveland, Baby daughter, Ross L., Roy R., Joseph Franklin, William Olin and Willie Lipham.

William Franklin Lipham "Buddy" suffered an attack of measles. One day he thought that he was well enough to go to the barn to feed stock in the rain; he subsequently died of pneumonia. William Franklin Lipham is buried at Pleasant Hill Cemetery in Harralson County near Tallapoosa, Georgia.

- **Letter from Belle Lipham Tuggle (1875-1970) to her great-Niece Mary Downs Smith, July 26, 1969**

Dear Mary,

I am sorry I can't give you much information you want, as I was only two months old when your mother **{Hettie**

Lipham Downs} was born. My mother {**Saphronia Davis Lipham**} took your mother and nursed her with me till she was two years old, when my brother {**William F. Lipham**} married the second time to **Charlotte Reaves**.

The only name I heard my mother call your grandmother {**Sara Vida Lee Lipham, 1856-1875**} was **Babe Lee**. She was buried in Randolph Co., AL near Franklin, GA. My brother William Lipham lived at that time near Franklin and moved to Haralson Co. GA when your mother was 2 years old. Your mother was a dear good woman and seemed more like a sister to me than a niece.

I am 94 years old now and very feeble. I would like for you to visit me. Love, AUNT BELLE

• **Excerpt from letter from Eleanor Johnson Eldredge to her sister Isabelle Johnson Whatley, then living in Washington, D.C.:**

Dear..Isabelle,

. . . While I was visiting her in Bowdon, **Aunt Mary {Downs Smith}** wanted to go down to Rock Mills, Ala., near Roanoke, to find some information on her mother's mother's people, the **Lee family**. Aunt **Ruby {Barwick Downs}** is trying to trace down family for Uncle **Charles Emory**'s side, so DAR eligibility can be verified. Uncle **Jim {Smith}** and Aunt Mary and Floy and the ubiquitous and ever-yapping MarJi went for a ride to very rural Georgia and Alabama. It was such a beautiful day to ride in the country, and we did find the right house after asking about six times. Mary said she had been there lots of times while she was growing up, and the last time she went was a few years before Grandmother **{Hettie Lipham Downs}** died. Mary carried her over there to see Uncle **Will Lee**.

Of course he has since died, but we talked to **Frank Lee**. Near as I can figure out he is Mary's second cousin, and the old graveyard was way behind his house. We could get to it easily; every thing was cleared out and it certainly wasn't weedy looking. Not a one of the gravestones was sunken or broken or knocked over. But the most recent one must have been 1903, and they were granite - and so overgrown with moss and lichen that most of it was completely illegible unless we had a stiff brush, or some chalk to outline letters or something. We worked real hard on the tombstone of Grandmother's mother **{Sara Vida Lee Lipham, 1856-1875}** who died giving birth to her at 22 years old. Frank Lee said this was put on her tombstone at her own request, and we finally were able to make it out:

In Memory of Sara V. Lipham
Daughter of I. B. & M. A. Lee
Born Mar the 29, 1856
Died Oct the 8 1875
Remember Friend
As you pass by,
As you are now
So once was I,
As I am now
you soon will be,
So prepare on earth
And follow me.
Sweep around
My Grave
Every fourth
Saturday Evening.

I have had a letter from Aunt Mary since, and she was delighted that **Phronia Lipham** had sent her a lot of material on that side of the family dating back to 1610. Can you imagine. Mary said she had it all copied and was sending it back to Cousin Phronia in Tallapoosa. Mary has already subscribed to some geneaology magazine. She is real interested in it, but she said she knows very well Aunt Ruby is content to copy out what is in the family Bible, and let Mary do all the leg work, visiting cemeteries and courthouses. I

think it is real interesting, and I wanted to read all the tombstones but it was growing late. Uncle Jim was in a hurry as usual. . .
{end of quote}
- **By Jeanne Whatley Baldwin and posted to Find A Grave in 2008.**

Charlotte Stewart Merrill Reaves Lipham was born Oct. 8, 1852 and died Feb. 23, 1928. She was widowed twice; lost 5 babies in infancy. Raised large family; built house alone. First husband Elliot C. John Reaves 1850-1872. 2nd husband William Franklin Lipham 1855-1889.

In 1877, widower William Franklin Lipham married Mrs. Charlotte Reaves, a widow with a son Herman, age six. William, or Buddy as he was known, brought his motherless two-year-old Hettie to the marriage. Charlotte, said to be of Irish descent, delivered ten Lipham children in twelve years, only five of whom lived. When 34-year-old William died of pneumonia in 1889, she was left to care for all these children and to complete the half-built Lipham home in Bowdon, which is still inhabited in 2008.

At age 75, and despite the surviving two daughters and three married sons, Charlotte chose to live at the home of step-daughter Hettie during her final illness. She would allow no one but Hettie to care for her. She died Feb. 23, 1928, at the Hettie and George L.

Downs home, in the "Pink Room," Bowdon, GA. She is buried at Bowdon United Methodist Church cemetery, next to her father Robert Edward Merrill.

Eleanor Johnson Eldredge was age seven when she died, but remembers hearing family members speak of Charlotte's illness - how she vomited up "coffee grounds."

Mary Downs Smith told Eleanor that Grandma Lipham kept a trunkful of cash, which she loaned out at interest. She saw it herself when being given candy from the trunk by Grandma Lipham.

- Clipping from unnamed newspaper - probably the <u>Bowdon Bulletin</u> c. Feb. 24, 1928:

Mrs. Charlotte S. Lipham Laid to Rest

Mrs. Charlotte S. Lipham, age 76, died at the home of her daughter, Mrs. G. L. Downs, on last Monday. She had been in declining health for more than six years. Throughout the entire time, she had borne her illness with fortitude and patience.

Mrs. Lipham was born and reared near Lamar in Randolph County, AL. She was married to Elliot J. Reaves in 1871. To which union there was born one child. Mr. H. J. Reaves. Following the death of her husband,

she was united in marriage to mr. W. F.
Lipham in 1878.

      Mrs. Lipham is survived by the
following children: L.C., W.O., C.M., Mrs.
W.T. Beck, Mrs. J.D. Muldrew, and Mrs. G.L.
Downs. She was a consistant member of the
M. E. Church, South for a long number of
years. Funeral services were conducted at the
M. E. Church, South on Thursday morning by
Rev. O. J. Withrow. Her many relatives and
friends mourn her passing, for she was
beloved by all.

- ## IN LOVING REMEMBRANCE OF W. F. LIPHAM

-       Oct 1889 , Carroll County, Ga
-       From copy of Funeral card:

IN LOVING REMEMBRANCE OF W. F.
LIPHAM,
Born Sept. 12, 1855
Died Oct. 25, 1889
Age 34 yrs. 1 mo. 13 days.
He has gone from his dear ones, his
children, his wife,
Whom he willingly toiled for, and loved as
his life.
O God! how mysterious and how strange
are thy ways,

To take from us this loved one in the best of his days.

1872 – William Franklin Lipham – abt. 17 yrs old

William Franklin Lipham

**William Franklin Lipham
Pleasant Hill Cemetery**

William Franklin Lipham

Sarah V. Lipham Lee
Lee Cemetery
Randolph County, Alabama

Old Lee Family Home

- **Built about 1890 by William F. Lipham and Charlotte Merrill Reaves Lipham. William did not live to see it completed, but Charlotte finished it and made it home to their nine children. This picture was made Aug. 2006.**

**Charlotte Merrill Reaves
Lipham – 1915**

Martha Sarah Etta "Sallie" Lipham
Daughter of Sarah Sophronia Davis
Grandchild of Joshua Davis
Great-Grandchild of William Henry Davis
September 29, 1857 – DOB
December 3, 1906 – DOD

Martha Sarah Etta Lipham, also known as Sallie, was the daughter of Sarah Sophronia and John Monroe Lipham. Sallie was born in 1857 in Georgia.

On December 2, 1894, Martha Sarah Etta married Arwidson Adolf Pittman. Arwidson was born in 1854 and died in 1943.

Per records, Martha Sarah did not have any children of her own but she did raise step-children.

Martha Sarah died in 1906 in Polk County, Georgia.

Martha Sarah Etta is the lady in the top row sitting in between her brother and her father, John Monroe Lipham. – 1905

- **Obituaries of Sallie Lipham Pittman 1857-1906**

  - **1906 , Polk County, GA, USA**
  - Part of an unidentified clipping found in the possessions of Mary Lipham Treadaway:
    - Mrs. Sallie Lipham Pittman was baptized into the fellowship of Bethany Baptist church, near Tallapoosa, and was married to Elder A. A. Pittman, December 2,

1894. She was the most industrious woman in Polk County. By making beautiful fans and brushes of feathers, hard work and economy, she saved some money and she requested a part of it to be given to build a church at Berry's Station, and to missions and the Orphans' Home. As a daughter, she was dutiful, affectionate and helpful, often relieving her father of the care of business affairs. As an associate, trustworthy and genial. As a wife, she was truly a helpmeet for her husband in every department of life. In governing her step-children she was firm and unyielding in what she thought was right. As a Christian, she was faithful, being a great lover of old sacred harp music. She was an unusual admirer of flowers, fowls and good cows. Her life was a victorious success, and her death a glorious triumph. Realizing fully a few days before the near approach of her last hour, she called her husband to her and kissed him farewell. She went away December 2, 1906, age forty-nine years, two months and two days. Lime Branch church is poorer, her beautiful home is lonely, but heaven is richer. May the Lord give church and husband that grace which will enable them to acquiesce, without murmuring, in the will of our heavenly Father, and give the influence of the blessed Comforter to the dear bereaved loved ones.

From another newspaper of that time -- In Memory of Mrs. Pittman

• God in his all wise providence has deemed it best to remove from us one of the noblest women Georgia ever knew, Mrs. Sallie Pittman, daughter of John M. Lipham. While we regret to part with her, and our hearts are torn and bleeding on account of the separation, yet we are consoled with the thought that our Father in Heaven knows best. Early in life she made an open profession of faith and united with the Baptist church at Bethany. She loved her church, her prayers, her tears, her money, her faithful attendance testified to her fidelity and devotion. Never will the writer forget the service at Bethany. When my heart was so hard an opportunity was offered for prayer. Sallie Lipham, with tears in her eyes and trembling voice said "can't you go?" Wednesday, last, while l the church at Lime Branch, her lifeless form lay in a casket lavishly covered with beautiful flowers, amid the sobs and tear stained faces of friends and relatives, I could almost hear her invitation to "come on". To Sister Pittman we could truthfully apply the proverb "She looketh well to her household and eatest not the bread of idleness". As a business woman, she was a notable success. Industrious, energetic, painstaking and progressive, she had gotten together a goodly portion of this world's goods. Her will, made verbally was that a portion be sent to the Orphans' Home, that some go to help build a church, the remainder was left to husband, step-children and to her father's family. Death was a welcome messenger to her. Just before dying the angels waited her spirit to Heaven and brought her back to bid her dear ones good-bye. She said, "I saw Mother and Sister Tommie,"* who had gone on before her. This precious sister shall no more walk the pathways of earth, her voice shall be heard no more among us, but let us not grieve as having no hope for we feel that our loss is her eternal gain.

*Her mother Saphronia Davis Lipham died in 1904; her younger sister Tommie Lipham Harris in 1894.

Emma Jane "Jennie" Lipham
Child of Sarah Sophronia Davis
Grandchild of Joshua Davis
Great-Grandchild of William Henry Davis
December 1, 1859 – DOB
March 4, 1946 – DOD

Emma Jane Lipham was the daughter of Sophronia Davis Lipham. She was born in 1859 in Heard County, Georgia.

On March 16, 1879, "Jennie" married John R. Driver. John was born in 1849 and died in 1922.

Per records, "Jennie" and John had the following children: Beulah, Floyd Monroe and John Bruce Driver.

Emma Jane "Jennie" Lipham died in 1946 in Dallas, Texas.

• **Grateful thanks to Clarice Sprewell Cox for this caption, which she published in her 1987 book LIPHAMS OLD YOUNG AND INBETWEENS, p. 58. (Library of Congress Catalog Card # 87-71976)**

Emma Jane Lipham, known to family and friends as "Jennie", was born in Heard County, Georgia 1 December 1859. She was married to John R. Driver in Haralson County,

Georgia 16 March 1876. They lived in Haralson County until about 1900, when they moved to Dallas, Texas, where they lived the remainder of their lives.

John R. Driver was a real estate dealer and was a man of substantial means when he died on February 16, 1922. He was first buried Oakland cemetery, but was later removed to Grove Hill Memorial Park in Dallas. Emma Jane "Jennie" Lipham Driver died in Dallas, 4 March 1946 at the age of eighty-six years. She is buried at Grove Hill Memorial Park in Texas.

1896
John R. Driver, Beulah, Floyd
Monroe, John Bruce and Emma
Jane "Jennie" Lipham Driver

Emma Jane Lipham Driver
Grove Hill Memorial Park in
Texas

Mary Saphronia "Babe" Lipham
Child of Sarah Sophronia Davis
Grandchild of Joshua Davis
Great-Grandchild of William Henry Davis
March 20, 1862 – DOB
August 4, 1960 – DOD

Mary Saphronia "Babe" Lipham was the daughter of Sarah Sophronia Davis. "Babe" was born in 1862 in Heard County, Georgia.

On December 5, 1886, "Babe" married Thomas Jackson "Jack" Treadaway in Haralson County, Georgia. Thomas was born in 1859 and died in 1897.

Per records, "Babe" and "Jack" had the following children: Bennett Whitfield, Charles Franklin, Mary Belle and Avis Pearl Treadaway.

Mary Saphronia died in 1960 in Carrollton, Carroll County, Georgia.

- ## How Aunt Babe Lipham Treadaway got her Nickname

  - 1862 , Tallapoosa, Haralson Co, GA

Aunt Babe was born during the Civil War and her father was away.

Family lore has it that the family wanted to wait for his return before

naming the new baby, so she was simply called "Babe" for some period of time, and the name just stuck.

She was also called Frony.

• Treadaway Family: Jessie, standing (she is Jack's daughter by his first wife), Frank at left, Bennett, and baby Mary Belle. A gracious thank-you to Clarice Spruell Cox for this picture, which she published in her book LIPHAMS, YOUNG, OLD & INBETWEEN, P.56, 1987, Library of Congress Catalog Card No. 87-71976.

Charles Wilson Lipham
Child of Sarah Sophronia Davis
Grandchild of Joshua Davis
Great-Grandchild of William Henry Davis
July 17, 1865 – DOB
June 14, 1938 – DOD

Charles Wilson Lipham was the son of Sarah Sophronia Davis. Charles was born in 1865 in Randolph County, Alabama.

On May 11, 1893, Charles married Eugenie Frances "Fannie" Awbrey. Eugenie was born in 1870 and died in 1963.

Per records, Charles and Eugenie had the following children: Frances Ruch "Ruthy", Luram, Ida Lucy "Lou", Saphronia Belle "Fronie:, and Mildred Awbrey Lipham.

Charles died in 1938 in Tallapoosa, Haralson County, Georgia.

Charles Wilson Lipham
1905

- **Charles & Fannie Awbrey Lipham, with Saphronia "Fronie" Belle on her mother's lap; Ida Lou on Charles' lap; seated, Ruth & Lura.**
1904

- **Lipham Family Lot, Bethany Baptist Church, Tallapoosa, Haralson Co, Georgia**

•

- **Lipham Family Lot, Bethany Baptist Church, Tallapoosa, Haralson Co, Georgia**

C. Polina Thompson Lipham
Child of Sarah Sophronia Davis
Grandchild of Joshua Davis
Great-Grandchild of William Henry Davis
April 23, 1868 – DOB
May 14, 1894 – DOD

C. Polina Thompson "Tommie" Lipham was the daughter of Sarah Sophronia Davis Lipham. "Tommie" was born in 1868 in Heard County, Georgia.

On December 25, 1888, "Tommie" married John Wesley Harris. John Wesley was born in 1864 and died in 1949.

Per records, "Tommie" and John Wesley had the following children: William Franklin "Frank", James Robert and Maudie Lee Harris.

C. Polina "Tommie" died in 1894 and is buried at Bethany Baptist Church Cemetery in Tallapoosa, Haralson County, Georgia.

**C. Polina Thompson "Tommie"
Lipham Harris**

**John Wesley Harris, James
Robert, William Franklin and C.
Polina Thompson "Tommie"
Lipham Harris
1892**

Ada Lipham
Child of Sarah Sophronia Davis
Grandchild of Joshua Davis
Great-Grandchild of William Henry Davis
May 4, 1872 – DOB
April 8, 1959 – DOD

Ada Lipham was the daughter of Sarah Sophronia Davis Lipham. Ada was born in 1872 in Randolph County, Alabama.

Around 1875, the Liphams moved from Alabama to Tallapoosa, Georgia in a buggy and covered wagon. Twins Ada and Ida, at the age of 3 years old, were in charge of keeping their feet on a strong box in the wagon which held all of their family's wealth.

On Easter Sunday, April 11, 1897, Ada married Dr. Oscar Henry Brock. The wedding took place in the home of Ada's father, John Monroe Lipham, near Tallapoosa, Georgia. Ada and her twin sister, Ida, were married to their spouses (who were twin brothers) in a double wedding ceremony.

Per records, Ada and Oscar had the following children: Thelma Gladys and Maurine Brock.

Oscar Henry Brock was born in 1874 and died in 1905. Ada Lipham Brock died in 1959 in Atlanta, Fulton County, Georgia. Ada Lipham Brock and Dr. Oscar Henry Brock are buried at Bowdon Methodist Protestant Church Cemetery in Bowdon, Carroll County, Georgia.

- On their wedding day in 1897, the two Brock brothers wed the two Lipham sisters in a double wedding at the home of the brides' father John Monroe Lipham.
- Dr. Thomas Whitfield Brock, Ida Lipham, Dr. Oscar Henry Brock and Ada Lipham on their wedding day.

Grave of Ada Lipham Brock (1872-1959), wife of Oscar Brock and mother of Thelmas Gladys Brock. Standing is George W. Johnson, great-grandnephew of Ada L. Brock.

The upright monument remembers Dr. Oscar Henry Brock, (1874-1905), husband of Ada Lipham Brock. Cemetery at Bowdon, Ga. behind the high school. The flat stone is for Thelma Gladys Brock Coley (1898-1983), wife of Francis Marion Coley and daughter of Oscar Henry Brock.

-      inscription....Beloved husband and loving father We are so lonely without thee He trusted in God

Ida Lipham
Child of Sarah Sophronia Davis
Grandchild of Joshua Davis
Great-Grandchild of William Henry Davis
May 4, 1872 – DOB
December 15, 1961 – DOD

Ida Lipham was the daughter of Sarah Sophronia Davis Lipham. Ida and her twin sister Ada were born in 1872 in Randolph County, Alabama.

On Easter Sunday, April 11, 1897, Ida married Dr. Thomas Whitfield Brock. The wedding took place in the home of Ida's father, John Monroe Lipham, near Tallapoosa, Georgia. Ida and her twin sister, Ada, were married to their spouses (who were twin brothers) in a double wedding ceremony. Dr. Thomas Whitfield Brock was a dentist.

Per records, Ida and Thomas "Whit" had the following children: Velma, Howell Gilmer, Gladys, Oscar Whitfield and Florine Brock.

Ida Lipham Brock died in 1961 in Atlanta, Fulton County, Georgia. Dr.

Thomas Whitfield "Whit" Brock was born in 1874 and died in 1949.

Ida and baby Gladys - 1905

Dr. Thomas Whitfield Brock (Dentist) and Ida Lipham Brock

- **On their wedding day, the two Brock brothers wed the two Lipham sisters in a double wedding at the home of the brides' father John Monroe Lipham.**

Ida Lipham Brock, wife of Dr. Thomas Whitfield Brock Westview Cemetery in Atlanta, Georgia

Belle Lipham
Child of Sarah Sophronia Davis
Grandchild of Joshua Davis
Great-Grandchild of William Henry Davis
July 18, 1875 – DOB
April 29, 1970 – DOD

Belle Lipham was the daughter of Sarah Sophronia Davis. Belle was born in 1875 in Randolph County, Alabama.

On June 25, 1902, Belle married Robert Jesse "Bob" Tuggle in Tallapoosa, Haralson County, Georgia. Robert was born in 1866 and died in 1912.

Per records, Belle and Robert had the following children: John Robert, Vera Louise, Jennie Mae and Robert Jesse Jr. Tuggle.

Belle died in 1970 in Atlanta, Fulton County, Georgia.

Dear Aunt Mildred,
. . . While in Atlanta I also visited Aunt Belle **{Lipham Tuggle}**- 93 years old. She is a little hard of hearing and is arthritic, but I was amazed that she seems alert and responsive at that age.

She keeps up with her rental collection to exist - from conversation I gathered this. Jennie Mae was at work and I did not see her. However, Vera is at home all the time, having been retired for 11 years. She is about 9/10's off her rocker was my impression.

But I'm real glad I went over there. Aunt Belle talked a lot about Grandmother - like a sister. She is 2 months older than Grandmother **{Hettie Lipham Downs}**. . .

**Robert Jesse "Bob" Tuggle and
Belle Lipham Tuggle**

Belle Lipham Tuggle
Hollywood Cemetery
Tallapoosa, Georgia

Robert Jesse Tuggle
Wife of Belle Lipham Tuggle

Lewis Franklin Davis III
Child of Wilson Lumpkin Davis
Grandchild of Joshua Davis
Great-Grandchild of William Henry Davis
1859 – DOB
July 23, 1908 – DOD

Lewis Franklin Davis III was the son of Wilson Lumpkin Davis. Lewis was born in 1859 in Georgia.

On November 16, 1879, Lewis married Laura Cervana Baird in Heard County, Georgia. Laura was born in 1859 and died in 1910.

Per records, Lewis and Laura had the following children: Thomas Wilson, Mattie Lorena, Edward Charles, James Grady, Etta Lee, Dora Alice, Winnie Ora, Lewis Owen, Albert and Alfred Allen Davis.

Lewis Franklin Davis III died in 1908 and is buried in China Spring Cemetery in China Spring, Texas.

Lewis Franklin Davis III
China Spring Cemetery in Texas

Elizabeth Davis
Child of Richard Bines Davis
Grandchild of Samuel Davis
Great-Grandchild of William
Henry Davis
September 25, 1861 – DOB
December 16, 1934 – DOD

Elizabeth Davis Williams
was the daughter of Richard Bines
Davis. Elizabeth was born in 1861 in
Sanderson County, Baker, Florida.

On February 18, 1885, Elizabeth
married General Jackson Williams in
Baker Florida. General Jackson was
born in 1863 and died in 1928.

Per records, Elizabeth and
General Jackson had the following
children: Annie, Rosetta (Rosa),
Sidney Samuel, Hardy, Linnie Leona,
Edward, Sottia, Altie, Claudia, Flossie,
Alva Jackson, Lee Ernest, Luverna Lou
and Lawrence Williams.

Elizabeth Davis Williams died in
1934 in Lake City, Columbia Florida.

**General Jackson and Elizabeth
Davis Williams**

John Thomas Faver
Child of Caroline Amelia Davis
Grandchild of Lewis Lanier Davis
Great-Grandchild of William Henry Davis
September 13, 1835 – DOB
September 20, 1906 – DOD

John Thomas Faver was the son of Caroline Amelia Davis Faver. John was born in 1835 in Wilkes County, Georgia.

On September 2, 1855, John Thomas married Amanda M. Stephens. Amanda was born in 1839 and died in 1879. Per records, John Thomas and Amanda had the following children: Louisa Ann, William Allen, Mary E., Isabella, Lewis, Isiah, Callie, Velitha Caroline, Minor Sanders, Bettie Lou and Susan Faver.

John Thomas Faver died in 1906 in Gilmer, Upshur Texas.

John Thomas Faver

Louisa Ann Faver
Child of Caroline Amelia Davis
Grandchild of Lewis Lanier Davis
Great-Grandchild of William Henry Davis
October 9, 1837 – DOB
July 20, 1910 – DOD

Louisa Ann Faver was the daughter of Caroline Amelia Davis. Louisa was born in 1837 in Wilkes County, Georgia.

On January 10, 1856, Louisa married John Thomas Vaughan. John Thomas was born in 1836 and died in 1864. No children are recorded for Louisa and John Thomas.

On August 15, 1867, Louisa married John Wingfield Terrell Gibson. John was born in 1843 and died in 1917. Per records, Louisa and John had the following children: Harriet, Ada, Mary, Brenda, Joel Jacobus, Sarah "Sallie", John Sanders and Caroline Louisa "Carrie Lou" Gibson.

Louisa Ann died in 1910 in Coweta County, Georgia.

**Louisa Ann Faver Gibson
1870**

**Louisa Ann Faver Gibson
1893**

Teresa Faver
Child of Caroline Amelia Davis
Grandchild of Lewis Lanier
Davis
Great-Grandchild of William
Henry Davis
April 7, 1845 – DOB
October 12, 1928 – DOD

Teresa Faver was the daughter of Caroline Amelia Davis. Teresa was born in 1845 in Centralhatchee, Georgia.

In 1862, Teresa married Issac Newton Davis Stephens in Heard County, Georgia. Issac was born in 1841 and died in 1924.

Per records, Teresa and Issac had the following children: William R., Johnnie Jeptha, Issac Eugene, Ida Lila, Minor Marlin, John L., Viola Caroline, Myra Melissa, Minnie Teresa and Richard Benjamin Stephens.

Teresa Faver died in 1928 in Judson, Texas.

Teresa Faver Stephens

Teresa Faver Stephens

Issac Newton Davis Stephens

INDEX

John Henry Davis 1833-1911
Elizabeth Davis 1793-1859
James Gresham Davis 1796-1846
Mary Christian Polly Davis 1800-1831
William Owen Davis 1800-1847
Nancy Ann Mourning Davis 1802-1887
Judith Leake Davis 1804-1878
Martha Frances Davis 1813-1870
Mary Gresham Davis 1798-1850
Catherine Davis 1803-1845
James Gresham Davis 1806-1867
John C. Davis 1806-1867
William Columbus Davis 1809-1886
Elizabeth Davis 1811-1882
Harriett L. Davis 1813
Tabitha Frances Davis 1815
Sarah Jane Davis 1818-1892
Joshua LT Davis 1823-1867
Judith Agnes Davis 1826-1872
James Chamberlain Davis 1812-1812
Lewis Franklin Davis 1817-1857
Mary Amanda Davis 1818-1849
William Thomas Davis 1820-1860
Martha Emiline (Lina) Davis 1823-1898
Rebecca Balsora Davis 1826-1905

Sarah Sophronia Davis 1830-1904
Wilson Lumpkin Davis 1833-1914
Richard Bines Davis 1817-1891
Caroline Amelia Davis 1819-1899
Ann Cordella Davis 1820-1872
Isaiah Tucker Davis 1822
William L. Davis 1824
Andrew J. Davis 1826
Isabella Davis 1828
Nancy Davis 1829
Edward Davis 1831-1912
Samuel Webster Davis 1836-1905
Hezakiah Kirah Davis 1851-1876
Elizabeth Jane Davis 1830-1906
James Franklin Davis 1832-1894
Morgan M. McLeod 1848-1918
John Noble Davis 1868-1956
Mary Cryssa Davis 1882-1978
Ardelia May Davis 1887-1919
William Davis Beck 1825-1871
Fredonia Ann Beck 1836-1862
George Granberry Davis 1840-1917
Charles G. Lyle 1837-1929
James Davis Lyle 1844-1930
Martha Melissa Davis 1841-1908
Mary Elizabeth Davis 1844-1907
Martin Joshua Davis 1845-1916
William Owen Davis 1847-1941
Lewis Franklin Davis Jr. 1849-1938

Andrew Smith Davis 1856-1902
Peter Taylor 1848-1922
Nancy Smith Pittman 1855-1944
Etta Jane Pittman 1864-1946
William Franklin Lipham 1855-1889
Martha Sarah Etta Lipham 1857-1906
Emma Jane Lipham 1859-1946
Mary Saphronia Lipham 1862-1960
Charles Wilson Lipham 1865-1938
C. Polina Thompson Lipham 1868-1894
Ada Lipham 1872-1959
Ida Lipham 1872-1961
Belle Lipham 1875-1970
Elizabeth Davis 1861-1934
John Thomas Faver 1835-1906
Louisa Ann Faver 1837-1910

Thanks goes out to everyone who helped with the gathering of information for this book. It has been a long project that I have enjoyed. Whenever I get letters or information in the mail, it is like Christmas time for me all over again. I treasure all the pieces of information that has been shared throughout the years.

About the Author

My name is Ida Rebecca Kos. I am the daughter of Betty Jean Davis Lane and the Granddaughter of John Oscar Davis. Correction from my previous book: I am the Great, Great, Great, Great granddaughter of Lieutenant Colonel William Henry Davis and the Great, Great, Great granddaughter to Edward Davis. I have spent 30 years in researching my family's history! Old pictures and stories always amaze me.

Other books found at Barnes
and Noble

Branches, Twigs and Splinters
of Edward Davis

Branches, Twigs and Splinters
of Lieutenant Colonel William
Henry Davis

Upcoming book by January of
2017
Heavenly Homecoming
Davis/Bates Children

CPSIA information can be obtained
at www.ICGtesting.com
Printed in the USA
LVHW110946010922
727374LV00004B/36